T0329107

# Cambridge Elements ≡

Elements in Political Economy
*edited by*
David Stavasage
*New York University*

# NATIVISM AND ECONOMIC INTEGRATION ACROSS THE DEVELOPING WORLD

## *Collision and Accommodation*

Rikhil R. Bhavnani
*University of Wisconsin–Madison*

Bethany Lacina
*University of Rochester, New York*

CAMBRIDGE
UNIVERSITY PRESS

# CAMBRIDGE
## UNIVERSITY PRESS

University Printing House, Cambridge CB2 8BS, United Kingdom

One Liberty Plaza, 20th Floor, New York, NY 10006, USA

477 Williamstown Road, Port Melbourne, VIC 3207, Australia

314–321, 3rd Floor, Plot 3, Splendor Forum, Jasola District Centre, New Delhi – 110025, India

79 Anson Road, #06–04/06, Singapore 079906

Cambridge University Press is part of the University of Cambridge.

It furthers the University's mission by disseminating knowledge in the pursuit of education, learning, and research at the highest international levels of excellence.

www.cambridge.org
Information on this title: www.cambridge.org/9781108733908
DOI: 10.1017/9781108678063

© Rikhil R. Bhavnani and Bethany Lacina 2018

First published 2018

A catalogue record for this publication is available from the British Library.

ISBN 978-1-108-73390-8 Paperback
ISSN 2398-4031 (online)
ISSN 2514-3816 (print)

# Nativism and Economic Integration Across the Developing World

## Collision and Accommodation

DOI: 10.1017/9781108678063
First published online: August 2018

Rikhil R. Bhavnani
*University of Wisconsin–Madison*

Bethany Lacina
*University of Rochester, New York*

**Abstract:** Migration and nativism are explosive issues in Europe and North America. Less well known is the tumult that soaring migration is creating in the politics of developing countries. The key difference between anti-migrant politics in developed and developing countries is that domestic migration – not international migration – is the likely focus of nativist politics in poorer countries. Nativists take up the causes of subnational groups, vilifying other regions and groups within the country as sources of migration. Since the 1970s, the majority of less-developed countries have adopted policies that aim to limit internal migration. This Element marshals evidence from around the world to explore the collision of internal migration and nativism. Subnational migration is associated with a boom in nativist politics. Pro-native public policy and anti-migrant riots are both more likely when internal migration surges. Political decentralization strengthens subnational politicians' incentives and ability to define and cater to nativists.

**Keywords:** migration, backlash, nativism, discrimination, violence, immigration, urbanization, sons-of-the-soil, ethnic violence, globalization

ISBNs: 9781108733908 (PB), 9781108678063 (OC)
ISSNs: 2398-4031 (online), 2514-3816 (print)

# Contents

1 Globalization versus Nativism in Unexpected Places     1

2 Within-Country Migration and Nativism     13

3 Nativist Parties and Policies     33

4 Migration and Sons-of-the-Soil Riots     54

5 Integration and Nativism: Averting the Collision     70

References     85

# 1 Globalization versus Nativism in Unexpected Places

In Europe and North America, anger at globalization has reshaped politics. Populists blame free trade for deindustrialization and foreign entanglements for the decline of the welfare state. Their most potent grievance is against international migration and multiculturalism. The political power of anti-migration appeals became undeniable in 2016, when British voters narrowly opted to exit the European Union and Donald Trump won the US presidency. Hundreds of political observers have pointed out the backlash against global integration and against international migration in particular.[1]

Developing countries play a role in the anti-globalist narrative. Poor states supply the migrants who overwhelm the West. Investment and manufacturing are diverted to less-developed countries, further pinching the working class in the West.

Ironically, migration and nativism are also explosive issues in *developing world* politics.[2] Economic growth and globalization have changed population flows within and among poorer countries. The numbers of migrants within the developing world are orders of magnitude larger than the flow of immigrants from poor to rich countries.

The key difference between anti-migrant politics in developed and developing countries is that domestic migration – not international migration – is frequently the focus of nativists in poorer countries. Nativists take up the cause of subnational groups defined by ethnicity, locality, or both. They rail against central government policies that promote domestic economic integration and vilify other regions and groups in the same country as sources of unwanted migration. Such domestic nativism is common in the developing world and is likely to strengthen as markets become more integrated within and across international borders. Market integration, surging population movements, and internal nativism are on a collision course.

## 1.1 Millions on the Move

In international statistics, an *internal migrant* is someone who has moved between the "largest zonal demarcations in a country" (UNDP 2009: 21).

---

[1] The scholarly literature on this issue is vast (Irwin 2002; Scheve and Slaughter 2001). On the backlash against international migration in particular, see Margalit (2011) and Williamson (1998).

[2] Our argument applies to nonindustrialized countries and postcommunist countries. Most of these countries have economies classified by the United Nations as "in transition" or "developing." Our argument is least relevant in very rich states with large welfare programs, which ensure low spatial disparities in household income. These are countries in western and southern Europe, along with Australia, Canada, Japan, New Zealand, and the United States. We use "less developed," "developing," and "poorer" to refer to the countries to which our argument is applicable.

By that standard, there are over 760 million internal migrants in the world, or 10 percent of the global population. International migration is far more modest: a little more than 210 million people, or 3 percent of global population.[3] China alone may have more internal migrants than the total number of international migrants in the world (King and Skeldon 2010). Counting people who split their time between administrative regions in the same country would swell the statistics on internal migration further. For example, the 2007–8 round of India's national unemployment survey found that just 1 percent of rural house-holds had made a permanent move in the last year. However, 3 percent of rural males had spent between one and six months away from their village or town in search of work (NSS 2010).

Poorer countries have traditionally had less dynamic economies and lower rates of internal migration. However, the number of internal migrants in developing countries grew throughout the twentieth century, and that growth accelerated after 1990 (World Bank 2009).[4] The boom in internal migration reflects some of the same forces that have driven the global integration of markets. Falling transport costs and expansion of infrastructure have eased migration. Increasing movement reflects the demise of central planning in countries such as China, Russia, and Vietnam, all of which relaxed restrictions on internal movement as they liberalized. Internal migration has increased in countries that abandoned import-substitution industrialization, shifting invest-ment toward labor-intensive sectors (Lucas 2015). Climate change and envir-onmental disasters will become increasingly important drivers of internal migration.

Internal migration is also related to global urbanization. By 2030, urbanites will be in the majority in every region of the world (UNDP 2009). Almost all global population growth will occur in towns and cities of less-developed countries, which will reach a combined population of 5.3 billion people by 2050 (Montgomery 2008). Natural increase, not migration, is the number one source of urban growth.[5] Migration is hugely important, however. In Asia,

---

[3] Both domestic and international migration figures are likely underreported because states – particularly developing countries – lack the capacity to track people as they move across internal and external borders. This problem is worsened by the fact that people often have incentives to obfuscate whether they are migrants or not.

[4] There is debate as to whether this acceleration continues (World Bank 2009) or has leveled off (UNDP 2009).

[5] Statistics on urbanization tend to be based on government designations of certain areas as "urban" rather than criteria such as population density or nonagricultural employment. Potts (2012) points out that urban areas are sometimes defined using fixed population thresholds. If a country has a generally high birth rate, rural areas may pass the "urban" benchmark without taking on any other characteristics of urban settlements. Potts uses this point and other critiques to argue that urbanization in Sub-Saharan Africa is not increasing.

Africa, and Latin America, migration from rural to urban areas accounts for approximately 40 percent of urban growth (Faetanini and Tankha 2013: 3). Migration from rural areas to urban areas is a growing portion of all internal migration.

## 1.2 Discouraging Migration

Internal migration is generally thought to be good. Voluntary migrants benefit financially from their move and, in most cases, boost the host area's economy as well.[6] Social scientists link migration to responsive government. The threat of citizen exit constrains the government's abuse of power. Interjurisdictional competition for migrants can improve public policies (Tiebout 1956). Freedom of movement is also a human right, enumerated in many constitutions and in Article 12 of the International Covenant on Civil and Political Rights.

Notwithstanding these benefits, most developing countries deploy a range of formal and informal policies to regulate internal migration. In 2009, Freedom House recorded moderate to high barriers to internal migration and/or emigration in 47 percent of middle-income countries and 80 percent of low-income countries.[7] Governments tamp down on rural-to-urban migration in particular because of its myriad supposed negative effects:

> [P]olicy makers in many developing countries – particularly in South Asia and in Sub-Saharan Africa – have been conditioned by an early literature on migration to worry about the specter of rising urban unemployment, overburdened city services, social tensions in economically vibrant areas, and a "brain drain." (World Bank 2009: 147)

The threat of urban unrest also motivates restrictions (Bates 1981). The potential for collective action and contagion means that "large cities are dangerous for nondemocratic regimes" (Wallace 2013: 17). Kundu (2009) and Montgomery (2008) are skeptical that the world's urban population will ever reach the loftiest projections because governments are raising barriers to urban migration.

United Nations data suggest that official resistance to internal migration is increasing. Figure 1 is based on data from less-developed UN member states collected by the UN Department of Economic and Social Affairs (DESA). DESA (2015) tracks which countries have central government policies that attempt to change patterns of internal migration. The dots in Figure 1 are UN estimates of the percentage of less-developed countries with policies aimed at

---

[6] Lucas (2015); Mendola (2012); Zhu (2013); Housen, Hopkins, and Earnest (2013); World Bank (2009).

[7] Reported in UNDP (2009: Table 2.3).

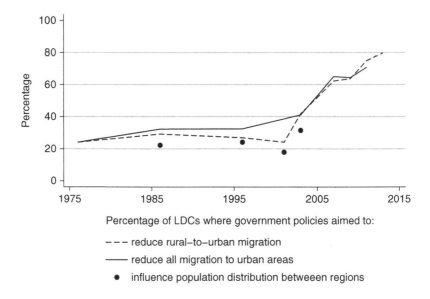

**Figure 1** Internal migration policies in less-developed countries, 1976–2013
**Source:** Based on DESA (2015).

"influenc[ing] the spatial distribution of population between regions within the country." The United Nations found these regimes in 22 percent of less-developed countries in 1986 and 32 percent in 2003. Restrictions on migration to urban areas – represented by the continuous line in Figure 1 – have exploded. In 1976, 24 percent of medium- and low-income countries had policies designed to reduce immigration to cities and rural-to-urban migration in particular. The prevalence of both kinds of migration policies soared starting in the mid-1990s. In 2003, 41 percent of less-developed countries sought to slow migration to urban areas. In 2011, the United Nations reported that 70 percent of these states intended to curtail migration to urban areas.

The recent surge in migration restrictions reflects domestic nativism. *Domestic nativism*, or *sons-of-the-soil politics*, is an antagonistic political response to the stresses of internal migration. Nativists argue that the interests of longtime residents of a jurisdiction should take precedence over the interests of new arrivals. India's Shiv Sena, one of the most famous sons-of-the-soil parties, encapsulates these ideas in its call for "Maharashtra [state] for Maharashtrians!"

The normative justification for anti-migrant policies is varied. Nativists may argue that longtime residents are indigenous, autochthonous, or claim religious or historical precedence. Others argue that the longtime population deserves to enjoy the fruits of their previous efforts to enrich an area. The variety of justifications for sons-of-the-soil rights go along with widely disparate time scales for defining natives versus migrants. Sino-Thais in southern Thailand are not the sons-of-the-soil, politically speaking, although their presence dates from at least the fifteenth century. By contrast, Gorkhas in Darjeeling, India, are the sons-of-the-soil in local politics, although most are descended from late-nineteenth-century migrants to the area (Lacina 2014).

The political view that recent migrants should be deprioritized relative to previous residents might also be referred to as *pro-indigenous, pro-local, anti-settler,* or simply *anti-migrant politics*. We use the term *nativism* (and sometimes *sons-of-the-soil*) because, first, nativist politics is not limited to places where the self-styled natives are indigenous by anthropological standards or to places where migrants are recently arrived. Second, terms such as *pro-indigenous* and *anti-settler* carry an ethical presumption in favor of locals and imply that the state is aligned with pro-migration forces.

> The term indigenous tends to be used for people who are already marginalised, while autochthonous is generally reserved for people who are dominant in a given area but fear future marginalisation. [Scholars] often sympathise with the former, while being highly critical of the latter. (Gausset, Kenrick, and Gibb 2011: 135)

Lastly, we argue that political institutions, including the degree of decentralization, influence whether migrants or nonmigrants are the marginalized population. For all these reasons, we try to avoid terminology that prejudges whether self-styled locals are marginalized or not.

## 1.3 Domestic Nativism

Local anxiety about internal migration is present across a variety of contexts: rural and urban, agrarian and industrialized, democratic and autocratic. In some instances, migrants are better off than natives and outcompete them in prestigious sectors. More often, migrants occupy a low place in the social and economic hierarchy. In either case, migrants embody change. Their presence feels to some like a threat to locals' way of life. Developers gobble up farmland. Laborers from the hinterland drive wages down. Squatters grab virgin lands. Shanty towns spring up and make city life squalid and crime-ridden. Strangers' children stuff public classrooms. Gauche condominiums overwhelm the water supply and power grid.

The stresses caused by subnational migration vary, but, on average, greater population inflows prompt the rise of nativist politics and policies. As migrants enter cities and compete with locals, politicians increasingly appeal to natives. They may do so by adapting existing party platforms or by launching new political parties. These appeals are electorally successful because migrants are frequently small in number and unable or unwilling to vote. Politicians therefore have strong incentives to cater to locals at the expense of migrants.

Migration prompts politicians to pursue sons-of-the-soil policies, especially in the labor market. Development experts recommend some policy responses to migration as best practices: investment in infrastructure, reduction of regional disparities in services, and natural disaster mitigation. Nativist policy is more narrowly tailored to privilege the interests of longtime residents over migrants and of members of ethnic groups that are ostensibly local over others. In spirit, sons-of-the-soil policies should be viewed "not as an attempt by government to find a solution to the tension between natives and migrants, but rather as an instrument by one group or another in the struggle to maintain or transform the ethnic division of labor" (Weiner 1978: 11). Sons-of-the-soil enthusiasts demand affirmative action and targeted spending in their favor, government discrimination against migrants, barriers to migration, and official harassment of migrants. Governments persecute or deport migrants and confiscate their houses or land. Some nativists will be anxious to deter, ban, or reverse migration. People who compete directly with migrants for jobs or natural resources are the most motivated to curtail migration. Others will simply want to ensure stable stratification of locals over migrants. This kind of nativism is attractive to people who purchase labor (e.g., day laborers, domestic employees) and benefit from a stream of migrants living at the margins of the economy and the political community.

Nativism manifests outside the realm of government policy as well. Firms may choose to favor locals in hiring. Consumers may direct spending toward local businesses and entrepreneurs. Property owners may refuse to sell real estate to outsiders. Nonstate discrimination against migrants is largely beyond the scope of this Element with the exception of one particularly costly phenomenon: the anti-migrant riot.

Riots against migrants can happen with or without the encouragement or forbearance of government actors.[8] There are clear instances of anti-migrant riots happening in defiance of the wishes of the state, for example, rioting by Tibetans against Han Chinese in 2008. There are enough cases of nativist violence by nonstate actors that, according to Fearon and Laitin (2011), almost a third of ethnic civil wars stem from such violence.

---

[8] A question that we cannot address in this Element is how a government that has decided to target migrants with violence decides what mix of official security forces and mob action to deploy.

[T]he spark for the war is violence between members of a regional ethnic group that considers itself to be the indigenous "sons-of-the-soil" and recent migrants from other parts of the country ... The violence often begins with attacks between gangs of young men from each side, or in pogroms or riots following on rumors of abuse (rapes, thefts, insults) or protests by indigenous against migrants. State forces then intervene, often siding with the migrants, and often being indiscriminate in retribution and repression against members of the indigenous group. (Fearon and Laitin 2011: 199)

Given this pattern of unrest in the developing world, it is important to examine whether growing domestic migration is associated with higher levels of rioting and violent protests. In coming sections we theorize about and investigate anti-migrant rioting by nonstate actors. In practice, the available data do not pinpoint the motives of rioters, whether migrants or locals initiated the violence, or the role of the state in encouraging, tolerating, or repressing violence.[9] While our empirical evidence on violence is broad-brush, our theorizing is explicitly about the relationship between migration and anti-migrant rioting by nonstate nativist actors. There is simply not room in this Element to cover all the forms of political violence that domestic migration might influence.

In the next subsection we argue that anti-migrant policies and riots are particularly relevant to this Element in light of an increasingly common institutional feature of developing countries: political decentralization. As we argue there, political decentralization enables nativism.

## 1.4 How Decentralization Enables Nativism

In Section 2 we explain why domestic nativism is a powerful force in the developing world. Compared with richer countries, developing countries tend to be more internally diverse and have stronger regional identities and greater spatial disparities in household incomes. Also, governments frequently cannot distinguish internal and international movement as a practical matter. Attacks on foreigners become attacks on domestic migrants and vice versa.

Internal migration creates opportunities for nativist politicians within new or existing political parties or factions. An increasingly common institutional feature in the developing world, political decentralization, enables this nativist boom. In the past fifty years, both developed and developing countries have undertaken extensive decentralization of policymaking, policy administration, and revenue collection. Political decentralization creates arenas where ambitious politicians can profitably appeal to local rather than national cleavages

---

[9] We are skeptical that these are useful questions to pursue through large-*n* empirical work.

(Posner 2005). Electoral arenas define politicians' constituents and nonconstituents. A useful way for politicians to capitalize on the stresses caused by internal migration is to call their constituents natives and to define interlopers as those who cannot vote locally. Decentralization strengthens the connection between migration and both the success of domestic nativist politicians and the implementation of sons-of-the-soil policies.

Pro-native public policy and anti-migrant violence are both more likely as internal migration surges. To some extent, however, resources for natives and state discrimination against migrants have the potential to substitute for violence against migrants, especially nonstate violence. If a government enforces a ban on migration, nativist violence by nonstate actors is unlikely. Such an effort is redundant. This logic is why Fearon and Laitin (2011) argue that nativist rebellions against the government do not occur when security forces side with locals against migrants.

Because policy and violence are alternative means of controlling and expelling migrants, decentralization has an ambiguous role in sons-of-the-soil violence. Decentralized political competition promotes sons-of-the-soil campaigning. Politicians who "own" the nativist issue have an incentive to sponsor violence to increase anti-migrant fervor (Wilkinson 2004). By contrast, political decentralization increases the odds that the government will implement sons-of-the-soil policies. Such policies deter future migration and signal to migrants that they will receive no help from the state. Nativists have less reason to organize migrant expulsions. The net effect of decentralization on nativist violence is therefore ambiguous. Decentralization unambiguously strengthens the relationship between migration and government adoption of sons-of-the-soil policies.

## 1.5 The Rise of Sons-of-the-Soil Politicians and Policies

The goal of this Element is to show a fraught confluence in the developing world. Internal migration is surging and being met with a rising tide of domestic nativism. The resistance to internal migration is a barrier to realizing the economic gains associated with labor mobility. Sons-of-the-soil pressures lead governments to restrict the human right of free movement. Domestic nativism can also be the impetus to discrimination, riots, pogroms, and civil war.

A substantial literature in international political economy focuses on the effects of international migration, but the effects of domestic migration are relatively understudied. Yet, in the developing world, such migration has an impact frequently akin to the effects of international migration in developed countries.

How does internal migration shape developing-world politics? In this Element, we use cross- and subnational data from a number of sources to show that internal migration prompts nativist reactions. Almost all existing works on this issue are single-country studies of contexts where internal migration does indeed prompt a nativist reaction. The sons-of-the-soil literature therefore "selects on the dependent variable," weakening our confidence that internal migration is truly met by a backlash across the developing world. To overcome this issue, we employ practically *all* the data on internal migration and the backlash to it that we can find. Figure 2 displays the twenty-eight countries with 650 subnational units on which the various analyses in this Element draw.[10]

In Section 3 we show how the Shiv Sena – India's most famous sons-of-the-soil party – grew in response to internal migration. The Shiv Sena endorses the right of Marathi speakers to be preeminent in the Indian state of Maharashtra, which has a population the size of Japan and contains the world's eighth largest city, Mumbai. Looking district by district, we find that population flows from other Indian states lead to more Shiv Sena candidates running in subsequent elections, a higher share of the vote won by the Shiv Sena, and a greater portion of seats captured by the Shiv Sena. In past research, we have shown that migration to one area of India can be predicted by natural disasters in other areas, weighted by the population affected and the distance between the disaster and the potential destination (Bhavnani and Lacina 2015). We use disasters in migrant-sending areas as an instrument for migration into the districts of Maharashtra to better isolate the causal effect of migration on Shiv Sena success.

In addition to examining the notorious Shiv Sena, we consider the growth of indigenous peoples' parties in South and Central America. Latin American indigenous parties are best known to foreigners for rejecting neoliberalism, but the most tangible elements of their party platforms are strengthening indigenous property rights (Plant 2002) and "state recognition of indigenous communities as politically autonomous units" (Yashar 1999: 92, 94). These measures help the local community manage its relationship with the central state, commercial interests, and migrants. Development and settlers have gone hand-in-hand in many indigenous areas. Has anxiety regarding internal migration played any role in the success of indigenous party appeals?

Building on a study by Rice and Van Cott (2006), we measure the growth in vote share of indigenous parties in Bolivia, Colombia, Ecuador, Guatemala,

---

[10] Depending on the constraints of the data, different parts of our analysis use different subsets of these data.

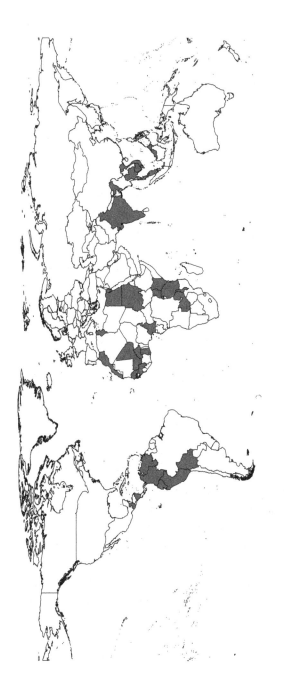

**Figure 2** Developing countries with available internal migration data used in this Element

**Note:** The twenty-eight countries with 650 subnational units used in our analyses are shaded.

Nicaragua, Peru, and Venezuela between the early 1990s and early 2000s. Indigenous parties grew most in areas that had higher levels of in-migration. This relationship is strongest in countries with elected subnational governments at the beginning of our period of study. This pattern is consistent with the expectation that political decentralization amplifies the relationship between migration and the growth of sons-of-the-soil parties.

We turn back to India for stronger evidence that decentralization strengthens nativists' influence over local policy. In 1993, the Indian central government adopted legislation that required the states to devolve greater power to district, subdistrict, municipal, and village governments and to create elected councils overseeing these substate governments. This experiment in decentralization, known in India as *Panchayati Raj*, was gradually rolled out across India's states over the next thirteen years, over hundreds of districts, and over hundreds of millions of people. The staggered introduction of district elections was due to the existing state election calendars, as well as lawsuits and budget shortfalls (Iyer et al. 2012). The timing of the introduction of substate elected governments was not related to the politics of internal migration.

Once a state established district-level elections, local bureaucrats became more accountable to sons-of-the-soil politicians. We use employment surveys – with almost a million native and migrant respondents from before, during, and after decentralization – to examine whether decentralization attenuated or magnified anti-migrant discrimination. Decentralization increased discrimination against migrants in government hiring. Prior to decentralization, migrants were as likely as nonmigrants to be employed by government. Once decentralization was in place, a gap in the rate of government employment between natives and migrants appeared. Decentralization shifted power in the local bureaucracy and the local economy to the sons-of-the-soil.

## 1.6 Migration and Violence

Nativists may adopt policies that restrict human freedom and economic development. Tensions over migration also carry the risk of violence. Section 4 shows that internal migration is positively correlated with rioting using a new sub- and cross-national database of internal migration spanning 526 regions in twenty-one countries in Asia and North and Sub-Saharan Africa. Furthermore, this correlation is particularly strong in places without decentralization, where local politicians arguably lack nonviolent means to assuage nativist demands.

There are reasons to be skeptical of a correlation between migration and rioting, not least because migrants take security into account when they make their moves. To address this issue, we use adverse monsoons in migrant-sending states to instrument for migration into India's states. When drought or deluge in other Indian states swells in-migration, the odds of rioting increase in the host state.

Lastly, we explore the ambiguous effects of decentralization on violence in India. Decentralization might incentivize politicians to rally natives against migrants, but local elections also enable pro-native policies. These policies can substitute for nonstate, anti-migrant violence, which is a more costly means of ensuring native primacy. We reexamine the staggered rollout of decentralization across Indian states, asking whether local elections changed the relationship between migration and violence. As described in the preceding subsection, this reform increased government discrimination against migrants, perhaps reducing the "need" for violence. Consistent with this argument, we find that the correlation between migration and rioting in India is weaker after political decentralization.

## 1.7 Conclusions

The collision between growing economic integration and nativism is destabilizing the developing world. It is easy to miss the parallel between these controversies and the anti-globalist populism of the West. The stress in developing countries is due to domestic migration and urbanization rather than international immigration. Anti-migrant sentiment is often labeled *nationalism* in rich countries, but this term is inapt in the politics of internal migration. By contrast, the term *sons-of-the-soil* commonly refers to nativism in poorer countries but not rich ones. We bring to light a common global struggle to accommodate the changes wrought by greater economic integration between and within countries. Everywhere, that transformation creates tensions between locals and new arrivals because these groups rarely play the same role in the economy or experience the same gains and losses from change.

One of the themes that runs throughout this Element is that nativism flourishes in diverse political contexts. The developing countries where we find examples of nativism vary on every dimension: size, diversity, region, urbanization, democratization, and recent economic trajectories. It is ironic that we find sons-of-the-soil politics in countries undergoing rapid economic growth and industrialization. Vignettes on nativist politics in the West emphasize the stagnation and deindustrialization of places such as western Pennsylvania and Manchester, England. We find nativist politics in the countries that have supposedly benefited from that decline. Economic change and economic competition are sufficient to produce nativist anxieties, even if the economy is not in an overall decline. Trends such as greater human migration and tighter integration of markets are truly global in scope, and the stress of responding to those changes is apparent in politics almost everywhere.

Nativism is a political barrier to development and a human security threat. This Element is a call for more attention to the conditions under which a backlash against internal migration can be avoided. Developing countries have a wider range of political institutions than rich countries, so the answer to the problem is unlikely to be simple. Our past research suggests that political parties play a role in mitigating nativism in India (Bhavnani and Lacina 2015, 2017), but parties are weak or irrelevant in many other countries. Even in India, the meaning and role of parties are in rapid flux. Finding the means to defuse internal nativism is both a complicated research problem and an urgent policy issue. In the developing world, surging population movements and economic integration are on a collision course with the politics of domestic nativism.

## 2 Within-Country Migration and Nativism

In practically all countries other than tiny, globalized states such as Singapore and Lesotho, domestic migration dwarfs international migration. Across these varied contexts, there are some common anxieties about internal migrants. Consider two ethnographic portraits of natives reacting to newcomers, one study from rural India in the 1970s and the second from metropolitan Kyrgyzstan at the turn of the millenium.

The indigenous ethnic groups of Chota Nagpur – which is now in Jharkhand state, India – are the Ho, Munda, and Oraon. They are "adivasis" or "tribals" in Indian parlance. Their ancestors predate Aryan settlement in northern India circa 1500 BCE. Starting in 1856, coal mining transformed Chota Nagpur, bringing infrastructure, industrialization, urban settlements, government bureaucracy, and a public education system. These facilities were overwhelmingly used and staffed by migrants. Miners and industrial workers, government staff, university students, and urbanites were primarily people from northern Bihar and Bengal. A tribal state assemblyman described tribal dispossession this way:

> The rise and fall of the adivasis ... depends on their land. If you take away their land they are like fish out of water. They do not want any other vocation in life. It used to be that half the land here was owned by the tribals as recently as the 1930s. Now, I think, it is only 25 percent. The tribals lost their lands to the new industries, especially to the Heavy Engineering Corporation. And then all the people who moved here took land from the tribals. Yes, the tribals were paid compensation, but what do they know about what to do with money? A Muslim or a Gujarati

> would know what to do with money, but tribals don't. So now the tribals
> have only the worst lands left. (Weiner 1978, p. 157)

In this account, migration is indistinguishable from economic transformation. Processes of development – urbanization, industrialization – make existing livelihood strategies untenable. The tribals lack the inclination and skills to participate in the new economy, which is ceded to newcomers. But the newcomers gobble up resources, destroying the old economy that the tribals would wish to continue.

Decades later, Bishkek, the capital of the Kyrgyz Republic, experienced a different transformation due to migration. The city grew from 620,000 to 835,000 residents between 1989 and 2009 (Hatcher and Thieme 2016: 2181). Newcomers came from northern Kyrgyzstan in the 1990s and from the south after 2005 (Flynn, Kosmarskaya, and Sabirova 2014). The combination of the new arrivals and out-migration from Bishkek to Russia reduced the Russian share of the city from 56 to 26 percent.

Comparatively speaking, Bishkek is not old. It grew from a fort to an urban area at the end of the nineteenth century in part due to Tsarist encouragement of Russian migration to the area. In 1926, the city, renamed Frunze, became capital of the Kirghiz Autonomous Socialist Soviet Republic. When migrants began to pour into the city in 1989, they were joining an ethnically mixed population that had passed just a few generations there.

The nouveau quality of Bishkek identity did not prevent anti-migrant sentiment against the population that arrived in the 1990s. Pre-1989 Kyrgyz-ethnicity urbanites identified more with the Russians than the newcomers, giving rise to the term "Kirgiz" to refer to Russified urban dwellers, in contrast to the rural "Kyrgyz" newcomers. Migrants built a sprawling ring of illegal settlements around Bishkek, with little access to public utilities, and worked in the undocumented economy (Thieme 2014). Hatcher and Thieme (2016) estimate that 20 percent of Bishkek's people are not registered with the city government, restricting their ability to "access basic urban services, to vote, obtain credit and formally set up a business" (p. 2177).

In 2008, a team of ethnographers asked some longtime urbanites for their memories of Frunze, as Bishkek was called under the USSR (Flynn, Kosmarskaya, and Sabirova 2014). Respondents compared the Soviet city to present-day Bishkek, arguing that the rural influx had undermined the quality of urban life.

> [Bishkek] is all southerners already … it is not the Bishkek it was, not the
> Frunze it was a long time ago … do you know what Frunze was like? It was
> such a clean, comfortable, green city, with such friendly people. It wasn't

terrifying at 12 o'clock at night to be out somewhere ... It was possible to walk through the whole of the city and nobody and nothing would bother you. (Flynn, Kosmarskaya, and Sabirova 2014:1516–17)

[Frunze] was so green. We would go to the cinema "*Rossiya*," it is closed now ... then it was such a huge cinema ... and those museums. I would go to the Frunze museum, to the park, everything was so beautiful ... and the fountains all worked. And it was so clean. I don't remember that in Frunze there was so much rubbish as there is now, there wasn't. And the people were completely different. They were all, or that's what it seemed to me, cultured. Earlier I didn't notice, and now everyone goes along, blowing their noses, spitting, and things like that. As we say, they have come down from the mountains and are here ... on the whole now the population is from the countryside, from the *kolkhozy* [collective farm]. (Flynn, Kosmarskaya, and Sabirova 2014: 1514)

Unlike the tribals in Chota Nagpur, these Bishkek locals are accustomed to urbanization. Unlike the tribals, longtime residents in Bishkek occupy a more prestigious and lucrative segment of the economy than the migrants (Allen 2003). Bishkek locals are not indigenous by the standards of Chota Nagpur, where tribes have lived for millennia. Bishkek is fairly new, and the population's history is one of recent migration and ethnic mixing. Despite the differences in economic situation and ethnic bona fides, a common thread binds the nativism of Bishkek's urbanites and the Chota Nagpur tribal assemblyman: the belief that migrant encroachment has made the locals' previous way of life impossible.

## 2.1 The Scope of Internal Migration

World over, and particularly in the developing world, the migration of people within countries is accelerating. Table 1 provides estimates of the total number of internal migrants by world region and the percent of the population those figures represent. Migrants are defined in two ways: the number of people who have moved between first-level administrative regions in their country in the last five years and the number of people who have made such a move since their birth. In Europe and North America, 5 to 7 percent of people shifted between administrative regions between 2000 and 2005. In Latin America, Africa, and Oceania, the flow of internal migrants in 2000–5 was 4 to 6 percent, not too far behind Europe and North America. In Asia, the percentage of the population migrating internally was more modest, about 3 percent. Translated into absolute terms, however, there were more than 100 million domestic migrants.

Rural-to-urban migration is a growing portion of migration but not the majority of internal migration. Migrants travel to areas where wages are higher

**Table 1** Internal Migration Worldwide, 2005

| Region | Past five years[a] | | Lifetime[b] | |
| --- | --- | --- | --- | --- |
| | Migrants (millions) | Percent of population | Migrants (millions) | Percent of population |
| Africa | 40 | 4.6 | 114 | 12.5 |
| Asia | 110 | 2.9 | 282 | 7.2 |
| Latin America | 22 | 4.1 | 100 | 18.0 |
| Oceania | 2 | 5.7 | 9 | 27.8 |
| Europe | 35 | 5.0 | 166 | 22.7 |
| North America | 21 | 6.8 | 92 | 27.8 |
| World | 229 | 3.7 | 763 | 11.7 |

[a] People who have moved between administrative units within the last five years.
[b] People living outside the administrative unit of their birth.
**Source:** Based on DESA (2013: Table 9).

or services are better than at their places of origin. Nonetheless, in Asia and Africa, most internal migration is between rural areas, from lagging to leading rural places (World Bank 2009). In Latin America, which is already quite urbanized, urban-to-urban migration is more common than rural-to-urban migration.

The most comprehensive and fine-grained source of internal migration data across the world is the Internal Migration Around the Globe (IMAGE) project (Bell et al. 2015). Recently released and publicly available, IMAGE's raw data allow for calculating average annual migration to subnational administrative units in fifty-five middle- and low-income countries. IMAGE has collected data from one census per country, providing a cross section from the 1990s and 2000s rather than a panel. For each country, we observe average annual migration into regions for five-year periods (and sometimes one-, two-, or six-year periods) in the 1990s and 2000s. For example, the data for Burkina Faso are from 2006, and the data for Cambodia are from 1994–98. We will use the IMAGE data in coming sections for our cross- and subnational analyses of the effects of internal migration.

Table 2 translates the IMAGE data into estimates of annual rates of internal migration, normalized by population. The sample includes twenty-one Latin American countries, seventeen northern and Sub-Saharan African countries, and fourteen Asian countries. IMAGE includes a number of European countries but just three – Estonia, Poland, and Ukraine – from

**Table 2** IMAGE Estimates of Annual Internal Migration
by Region

| Region | Annual internal migration as percent of population | Countries included |
|---|---|---|
| Africa | 4.5 | 17 |
| Asia | 5.1 | 14 |
| Europe | 0.7 | 3 |
| Latin America | 4.9 | 21 |
| Total | 4.6 | 55 |

**Source:** Based on Bell et al. (2015). For the list of countries, see Appendix Table S1.

the postcommunist world. The IMAGE data imply somewhat higher rates of internal migration than the DESA data presented in Table 1. For example, DESA found a five-year rate of migration in Africa of 4.6 percent. The IMAGE African countries had a similar rate of internal migration (4.5 percent) on an annual basis. IMAGE data likewise imply somewhat higher rates of migration in Latin America and Asia compared with what DESA observed. The three European countries we have taken from the IMAGE data set had very low rates of internal mobility in those data compared with the DESA data. The DESA Europe estimate includes the rich western European countries. In general, wealthier countries have higher rates of internal movement.

## 2.2 Migration and Competition

Economists expect that migration increases the efficiency of the distribution of labor.

> [L]abor migration contributes to aggregate growth by improving the distribution of labor, driving concentration. And by clustering skills and talent, migration drives agglomeration spillovers. (World Bank 2009: 162)

In the medium term, labor migration promotes regional convergence via remittances and faster national growth (Mendola 2012; Zhu et al. 2013; Housen, Hopkins, and Earnest 2013). Restrictions on internal migration, on the other hand, "create unnecessary friction and impose the cost of forgone opportunities for economic growth and convergence in living standards" (World Bank 2009: 147).

In theory, the gains from migration could be redistributed to ensure that all locals and migrants benefit from population flows. Efficiency gains could be used to offset two sources of friction in particular. First, internal migrants compete with the existing population for resources such as housing, clean water, and schooling.[11] Second, an influx of migrants expands the labor force – potentially lowering wages or leading to unemployment – at least in the short term. Both infrastructure- and labor-related stresses could be offset through taxation, public spending, and redistribution.

There are two reasons that the welfare gains due to migration might not be realized. The first is that some migration is not driven by better economic prospects. If a country has large disparities in public services, migrants may move in search of those services. Migration may also be induced by push factors such as environmental disasters, conflict, or inadequate support for rural development. In such circumstances, migration does not automatically produce gains via the efficient allocation of labor. Development experts recommend that governments eliminate or mitigate push factors such as service disparities across regions to manage internal migration.

A second bottleneck from realizing the economic gains from internal migration is a matter of governance. In a study of eight Asian megacities between 2003 and 2008, researchers found that migration increased cities' tax revenues (Satterthwaite 2008). The municipal governments did not use those revenues to address migrant needs. The municipalities were also not spending those revenues with an eye to compensating natives living with the stresses of migration such as overburdened utilities, higher housing prices, or lower wages.

> All cities and most smaller urban centers face a contradiction between what drives their economic development (and the in-migration this generates) and what contributes to adequate accommodation for the workforce on which they depend ... Cities grow as private investment concentrates there. But there is no automatic development of any capacity to govern the city and ensure that growing populations and economic activities can get the land, infrastructure and services they need ... Two characteristics shared by most Asian urban centers are the inadequacy in provision for the basic infrastructure and services needed in all residential areas – including provision for piped water, sanitation and drainage, roads, schools, electricity and health care – and the poor quality of the housing for large sections of the population. (Satterthwaite 2008: 6)

The researchers emphasized that city governments simply did not think of migration as a manageable policy challenge flowing from economic success.

---

[11]    Weiner (1978); Barnett and Adger (2007); Faist and Schade (2013); Homer-Dixon (1999); Swain (1993).

Governments saw the problems of infrastructure and public services as "'too many people moving to cities' [and] not as their failure to develop appropriate policies" (Satterthwaite 2008: 15).

Migration poses a challenge to many local governments, not just a few megacities. In the developing world, 40 percent of urban dwellers live in cities of no more than 1 million people (Montgomery 2008). In these cities, access to health and sanitation services is often comparable to that in rural areas. Smaller municipalities have more limited budgets, tax bases, and less access to experts and bureaucratic talent.

> Yet in an era of political decentralization, these smaller cities are increasingly being required to shoulder substantial burdens in service delivery and take on a larger share of revenue-raising responsibilities. (Montgomery 2008: 763)

Even rural areas have to manage the challenge of internal migrants seeking public services and putting pressure on resources. Markets for agricultural land are thin in less-developed countries, so it is virtually unheard of for a landed farmer to relocate voluntarily (Lucas 2015). Rural-rural migration is still the dominant mode of migration in the developing world, but due to landless laborers and movement to rural areas with relatively better services and access to national and international markets. Resource pressure due to rural-rural migration is a particularly important problem in Sub-Saharan Africa, where (unlike Asia) rural populations are still growing rapidly (Boone 2017).

Thus gains from migration are uncertain and unevenly shared. Mechanisms for sharing the gains from migration with adversely affected populations could exist but frequently do not. Without these measures, local support for open borders and migrant-friendly public policies flags.

In fact, there is deep public ambivalence about internal migration in many less-developed countries. The 1999–2001 wave of the European Values Survey (EVS) asked respondents to agree or disagree with the statement that "[w]hen jobs are scarce, employers should give priority to local people over people from other parts of the country" (EVS 2015: 231). This question was asked in eight low- to middle-income countries (Table 3). In every one, a clear majority of people endorsed hiring preferences for locals over internal migrants.[12] The rate of endorsement was lowest in Slovenia at 55 percent and highest in Croatia at 75 percent.

---

[12] Because this question does not state that internal migration yields efficiency gains, answers are arguably biased against migrants.

**Table 3** Endorsement of Preferences for Locals over
Internal Migrants in Postcommunist European
Countries and Turkey

| Country | Percent endorse preferences for | |
| --- | --- | --- |
| | **Locals** | **Citizens** |
| Croatia | 75 | 88 |
| Bulgaria | 75 | 88 |
| Poland | 71 | 91 |
| Russia | 70 | 73 |
| Ukraine | 69 | 70 |
| Turkey | 68 | 68 |
| Belarus | 60 | 85 |
| Slovenia | 55 | 76 |
| Greece | – | 78 |
| Austria | – | 74 |
| Germany | – | 64 |
| Great Britain | – | 59 |
| France | – | 54 |

**Source:** Based on the 1999–2001 wave of the European
Values Survey (EVS 2015).

For context, Table 3 also tabulates an EVS question on preferences for citizens over international immigrants. In most countries, preferences for hiring citizens were even more popular than preferences for hiring locals, although these measures were endorsed at roughly equal rates in Turkey, Ukraine, and Russia. In any event, supermajorities preferred both types of sons-of-the-soil privileges.

The demand for domestic nativism in less-developed Europe was on par with or even eclipsed the demand for anti-foreign nativism in Western Europe. The EVS asked people throughout Europe about hiring preferences for citizens over foreigners. The last lines of Table 3 tabulate the answers to this question for a few Western European countries where nativism is an important political issue: Greece, Austria, Germany, Great Britain, and France. Political observers agree that anti-foreign nativism is a powerful force in, for example, French politics. Fifty-four percent of French people endorsed anti-foreign hiring practices. In every lower-income European country, more than 54 percent of people wanted hiring practices that discriminated against *internal* migrants. In most cases, demand for internal sons-of-the-soil protections in Eastern Europe also eclipsed Germany's and

Great Britain's external nativism and was on par with that in Austria and Greece.

Like those living in the transitional economies of Europe, India's citizens share a strong consensus that subnational communities can and should discriminate against domestic migrants. A national survey in 2009 asked respondents to agree or disagree with the statement, "for jobs in [name of respondent's state], priority should be given to people from [name of respondent's state] over people from any other state." Seventy-two percent of respondents nationwide agreed, and the majority of respondents in every state agreed (Lokniti 2009). The subnational borders and governments of Indian federalism are understood by the public as a means of giving priority to nonmigrants.[13]

In Kenya, redrawing subnational boundaries was not enough to remove the expectation that local governments serve the sons-of-the-soil. The 2010 Constitution reorganized eight provinces into forty-seven counties with elected assemblies. The county-level civil service is over 100,000 strong, putting the counties in charge of a substantial block of local employment (NCIC 2016: xv). According to law, the counties are to give 30 percent or more of entry-level posts to applicants who are not from the locally dominant ethnic group. However, a 2014–15 audit found that only fifteen counties adhered to this rule, and the average county drew almost 80 percent of its staff from the locally dominant ethnic group (NCIC 2016: Tables 2 and 3). The auditors lamented that

> [t]he perception that counties were created for local people to wholly benefit from the financial, human and natural resources is misguided. This is aggravated by the fact that county policies such as flags seem to emphasize the indigeneity of certain groups within the county. (NCIC 2016: xvi)

The audit captures the popular presumption that counties should direct resources primarily to sons-of-the-soil. It also makes clear that politicians cultivated this expectation through symbolic gestures such as the design of county flags.

## 2.3 Nativist Policy

When migration increases, political entrepreneurs capitalize on the demand for anti-migrant, pro-native policy. Particularly in subnational politics, nativism is

---

[13] Because this question does not state that internal migration yields efficiency gains, answers are arguably biased against migrants.

frequently a winning strategy (Jha, Rao, and Woolcock 2007). Locals at least initially outnumber migrants. Locals are more likely to vote or have access to other levers of power. If incumbent politicians do not reduce local grievances in the face of migration, they risk being outflanked by upstart nativist movements or parties. The struggle between established parties and upstart nativists parallels the political response to international migration in parts of Western Europe, which has been linked to the rise of the right (Dancygier 2010).

Governments do not invariably side with natives and against migrants, of course.[14] Perhaps the government is inept, distracted, or committed to laissez-faire economics. Or the government may openly favor migrants, perhaps if they are from a dominant ethnic group. Regional governments in migrant-sending areas may maintain a stake in the well-being of their in-country diaspora. Central rulers sometimes believe that parts of their territory are economically underutilized or that overcrowding in one area can be relieved by movement to a less dense periphery. Governments sponsor migration of their supporters – defined in partisan or ethnic terms – to areas deemed insufficiently loyal to the capital. Beijing's encouragement of Han Chinese migration to Tibet is a well-known example. When the government wants a particular species of internal migration, the power of the state is with those settlers.

However, most developing countries are currently experiencing surging internal migration without the help of pro-migration governments. In fact, UN data (Figure 1) suggest that most governments are trying to curb internal migration to some extent. Migration increases are the result of globalized changes in technology and economic policy. In these circumstances, governments are not likely to have a firm commitment to the interests of internal migrants. The political appeal of nativism is all the greater.

Nativist policies are interventions designed to benefit natives disproportionately, even at the expense of migrants. To reduce competition for resources, the government might expel migrants or deny them services. City governments use zoning rules and periodic slum clearance to discourage and purge migrants. Local authorities discriminate against new arrivals in service provision. For example, Feler and Henderson (2011) find that in the 1980s, Brazilian municipalities withheld water lines from some neighborhoods in hopes of curbing migration.

Politicians might target spending toward natives, as in the case of Malaysia or South Africa, where government programs redistribute resources to locals.

---

[14] Gaikwad and Nellis (2017) describe the conditions under which politicians court migrants. See Auerbach (2016) and Thachil (2017) on the political behavior of migrants.

Targeting may also be implicit, when spending is directed to regions with fewer-than-average migrants. Quotas or explicit preferences for sons-of-the-soil crop up in public and private hiring, education, and legislative representation. These programs are sought after by natives because they provide a stream of benefits rather than a one-time windfall and are difficult to repeal (Bhavnani 2017; Bhavnani 2009). From politicians' perspective, such programs provide incentives for people to continue to identify as natives (Acemoglu and Robinson 2001). Governments can also implicitly sanction discrimination by private actors. Such strategic nonresponses (or "forebearance"; see Holland 2016) might discourage migration in the long run. At the extreme, governments might allow vigilante groups to repel migrants through violence (Bhavnani and Lacina 2015). In India, states pinched for fiscal resources to assuage nativists are more likely to allow and foment migrant purges (Bhavnani and Lacina 2017).

## 2.4 Nativist Riots

Migrants frequently live on the economic and social margins of their new homes. They are often targets of state harassment and coercion. A "government may be willing to tolerate and even generate ethnic strife if it serves to reduce migration or reduce the flow, or to bring about compliance with policies intended to change the ethnic division of labor" (Weiner 1978: 11). Migrants are rarely in a position to resist if the state attacks them or stands aside while they are targeted by locals.

> Why don't the migrants rebel if the state sides with the indigenous? ... For one, immigrants lack a rural base in which to hide from state forces, get support from noncombatants, and receive protection from neighbors who are tied together in dense social networks ... Second, compared to the indigenous population, migrants have a relatively cheap alternative to war: exit to their home area. (Fearon and Laitin 2011: 206)

Migrants rarely muster a rebellion in defiance of a government.

Violence by migrants against natives does occur when migrants are acting as an extension of the state or at least with the state's reluctant protection. This is the pattern familiar from European settlement in the Americas, Oceania, and southern Africa. When migration is blessed by a government, native resistance is likely to be met with state violence or state forbearance in the face of settler violence. State-sponsored migration can be coercive, violent, and even genocidal.

Nonstate anti-migrant violence falls between the two poles just described. At one extreme, a government directs state violence against migrants. At the other extreme, migrants are the tip of a government spear aimed at indigenous populations. During nativist anti-migrant riots, the alignment of the state is often ambiguous, at least initially. Perhaps the government is divided: some state agents may be encouraging and abetting violence, others ignoring it, and still others are inclined to repress the rioters. Or the state response may simply be slow to materialize. Sons-of-the-soil riots and protests present the state with the problem of choosing a side in a nativist-versus-migrant clash of interests.

Nativist riots outside the purview of the state are important because locals-versus-migrants clashes can escalate into much more extensive anti-state violence by the natives. Fearon and Laitin (2011) count thirty-one sons-of-the-soil civil conflicts between 1945 and 2008 in which natives fight against settlers, who are either backed by the government or who are newly vulnerable after losing government support (Boone 2017).[15] They argue that "the violence often begins with attacks between gangs of young men from each side, or in pogroms or riots" (p. 199).

An example of native-versus-migrant rioting metastasizing to civil war comes from Mindanao in the Philippines. Mindanao is the Muslim-majority southern region of the Philippines. After 1946, Manila sponsored large numbers of Christian settlers to Mindanao. In 1971, the "Battle of Buldun" progressed from a nativist riot to sons-of-the-soil warfare in the manner Fearon and Laitin predict.

> [F]ighting broke out between the indigenous Muslim inhabitants and Christian loggers for reasons not made clear in reports of the incident. After some Christian loggers were killed in retaliation for the shooting death of a local Muslim official, Buldun was fortified by local Muslims in expectation of a counterattack. A detachment of the Philippine Constabulary advancing on the town was fired upon and its commanding officer killed . . .
> The Philippine Army arrived in battalion strength and Buldun was bombarded by artillery for four days, after which an ultimatum to surrender was issued to the townspeople. (McKenna 1998: 153)

Open war between Muslim separatists and the central government was underway within a few years.

We expect that greater migration leads to more nonstate anti-migrant rioting by nativists. In the coming decades, more and more governments will have to develop a security response to nativist unrest, which motivates our focus on this form of disorder. We also believe that political institutions in the developing

---

[15] Opposition to migration has been highlighted in ethnographic accounts of ethnic conflict in Ghana and Indonesia (Côté and Mitchell 2016), central India (Jeffrey, Sen, and Sen 2012), Sudan (Seymour 2010), and Xinjiang, China (Millward 2009).

world have an important role to play in the incidence of nonstate nativist riots. We will return to this point later.

## 2.5 Why Internal Migration?

Why is internal migration – as opposed to international migration – politically fraught in the developing world, whereas it is typically a nonissue in rich countries? The greater political salience of internal migration in the developing world cannot be explained by scale. In both poor and rich countries, internal migration is a much larger flow of people than international migration. Internal migration is also more common in rich countries than in poor countries because of better infrastructure, more integrated labor markets, and higher incomes.

Domestic migration in developing countries occurs under different structural conditions than domestic migration in developed countries. The first key difference is greater spatial inequality within less-developed countries. Economic production is highly concentrated in rich countries. Nonetheless, all areas of the country tend to converge in terms of household incomes and living standards thanks to mobility and state redistribution. The World Bank estimates that

> households in the most prosperous areas of developing countries – such as Brazil, Bulgaria, Ghana, Indonesia, Morocco, and Sri Lanka – have an average consumption almost 75 percent higher than that of similar households in the lagging areas of these countries. Compare this with less than 25 percent for such developed countries as Canada, Japan, and the United States. (World Bank 2009: 2)

Ironically, development tends to increase the spatial concentration of wealth in the medium term. Within-country economic disparities are widening in countries that have grown rapidly in recent decades, as in East and Southeast Asia. Within-country disparities in income also grew rapidly as postcommunist countries in Eastern Europe and Central Asia abandoned state planning. Domestic migration is fraught in developing countries because spatial disparities in opportunity and well-being are profound and growing.

Second, middle- and low-income countries are on average more ethnically diverse than rich countries. The variety of languages spoken and religions practiced is wider. The number of politically salient ethnic groups is greater. For example, researchers at ETH-Zurich (Girardin et al. 2015) peg the average number of politically relevant ethnic groups in highly developed countries at three with a range between one and eight. In less-developed countries, that average is five, and the number of politically relevant groups ranges as high as forty-four. Because of lower historical migration, ethnic groups in poorer countries are also more likely to be concentrated in a regional homeland. Girardin et al. (2015) find an average of four regionally concentrated ethnic groups in less-developed countries and an average of one and a half in richer countries.

Third, the furor over internal migration in developing-world politics reflects the blurred distinction between internal and foreign migration. Ethnic groups that span borders are the rule and not the exception (Adepoju 1984). In the Indian state of Assam, a Bengali speaker might be an illegal migrant from Bangladesh, a recent transplant from Indian West Bengal, or part of a family that has been in Assam for generations. Every country in Southeast Asia has both Chinese-ethnicity citizens and recent migrants from China. Although Yorubaland is split between Nigeria and Benin, Yoruba speakers now live throughout West Africa because of international migration. Governments often lack the capacity to distinguish between international and domestic migration or between recent arrivals and naturalized citizens.

Internal migration and international migration are politically inseparable because public policies aimed at curbing foreign immigration will curb internal migration and vice versa. For example, in 1969, the prime minister of Ghana announced that illegal aliens would have two weeks to leave the country. Adida (2014) recounts the ordeal of "Mary," an ethnic Yoruba born in Ghana. As an adult, Mary and her husband moved from northern to southern Ghana. She initially assumed that the government's Alien Compliance Order would not touch her.

> But when Ghanaians began harassing her and her family, she realized this was no joke . . . An official countdown to the December deadline was aired on the radio every day [and] Ghanaian police patrolled the streets to ensure Ghana's "aliens" were packing up their belongings . . . Mary's husband rented a car to Lagos; they left with her child and parents promptly before the December deadline. (Adida 2014: 2)

When ethnic groups span weakly enforced international borders, nativists define "foreigners" in terms of ethnic difference rather than legal niceties.

An even more dramatic illustration comes from Côte d'Ivoire. Booming cocoa production brought thousands of migrants to southern Côte d'Ivoire from other parts of the country and West Africa. When presidential elections were opened to multiple parties in 1990s, Laurent Gbagbo used anti-migrant grievances in the southwest as a natural entry point into politics. He championed "ivoirité" and a "new conception of 'strangerhood' [that] conflated immigrants from Burkina Faso (and elsewhere) with northern Ivoirian Muslims" (Côté and Mitchell 2016: 661). These tensions led to electoral violence in 2000 and civil war in 2002.

## 2.6 Institutions that Favor Nativism

Institutions shape the political salience of domestic migration. Many postcolonial and postcommunist countries have a history of regulating internal migration. Laws and policies that can be deployed against migrants are already in place or only recently lapsed. Also, the contemporary trend toward greater political decentralization means that subnational politicians' incentives and ability to define and cater to natives are increasing.

Countries that once used centralized planning frequently had internal registrations or passports that made it illegal for citizens to move without government permission and impossible for citizens to access services after an unsanctioned move (UNDP 2009). Russia, China, Vietnam, Belarus, and Mongolia used versions of this system. These migration restrictions were centrally designed. Now, however, the demand to keep and strengthen these systems is bottom-up.

In Russia, local government has kept internal migration restrictions alive. In 1925, Stalin reintroduced the Tzarist *propiska* system of internal passports to aid the collectivization of agriculture. After the Soviet Union fell, freedom of internal movement was recognized in the Russian Constitution. Yet some city and regional governments use the household registration system to prevent internal migrants from voting, enrolling their children in school, and using other public services. In Moscow,

> there is strong public support for a restrictive registration regime. Some of this support can be tied to racism. It appears, however, that the majority of support for a restrictive registration system in Moscow – among both local leaders and the public – comes from a perceived need to protect against the flood of migrants many fear would occur as a result of a removal of the restrictions. (Schaible 2001: 350–51)

In 1998, the mayor of Moscow affirmed that the restrictions would continue even after they were struck down by the Russian Constitutional Court (see also US Department of State 2016: 38).

Likewise, in China, internal migration restrictions survived the end of central planning because they had powerful subnational public support. A household registration system, the hukou, was a tool of central rationing, planned industrialization, and a means of preventing rural-to-urban migration. The center has attempted to relax the hukou while also moving control of the system to provincial and municipal authorities. The food and fuel rationing system that the hukou once supported no longer exists. Nonetheless, cities and provinces continue to be stingy with legal permission for migration (Chan and Buckingham 2008; Vortherms 2017).

> The hukou derived its stickiness and its suppleness long after the economic
> transition was well under way from the range of social and official groups
> that supported it, namely, most urbanites ... and the wealthier, magnet
> regions of the country. (Solinger 2014: 8)

Regional governments have used their newfound authority to shore up the hukou system so that most nonelite rural people cannot easily move to the city.

In postcolonial countries, internal migration has historically been regulated subnationally. Boone (2017) describes the ethnic homeland system of colonial Africa.

> Colonial administrative structure and practice in much of twentieth-century
> Africa aimed at creating monoethnic rural districts (tribal homelands under
> colonial indirect rule). (Boone 2017: 278)

These homelands have an enduring imprint on identity, defining indigenous versus not: "[w]hat modern African states and demographers recognize as 'interethnic migration'" is movement between the colonial homelands (Boone 2017: 278). They also persist in law, determining land rights.

> Many postcolonial governments maintain prohibitions against the perma-
> nent sale of neocustomary land to ethnic outsiders, and almost all do so
> implicitly by not recording or enforcing land sales in zones of neocustomary
> tenure ... levels and rates of in-migration are controlled by ethnic insiders.
> (Boone 2017: 280)

Boone estimates that 90 percent of all land in Sub-Saharan Africa is controlled through these sons-of-the-soil institutions. Colonial homelands have parallels in parts of postcolonial Asia. India, Bangladesh, and Pakistan all have "tribal" tracts, originally designated under colonialism, where particular ethnic groups have special privileges. Migrants cannot fully take part in the economy of a tribal tract. The most important restriction is usually a ban on selling land to migrants. In India, the federal states also have the power to create sons-of-the-soil preferences in state hiring and education.

### 2.6.1 The Simultaneous Boom in Political Decentralization

Growing domestic migration across the developing world is happening alongside a worldwide trend of increasing decentralization. Decentralization takes many forms, including administrative and political decentralization. Administrative decentralization aims to redistribute government authority to new lower tiers, or new units within tiers, of government. Political decentralization aims to give elected, rather than centrally appointed, politicians greater responsibility over subnational governments (Rodden 2005). In Figure 3, we

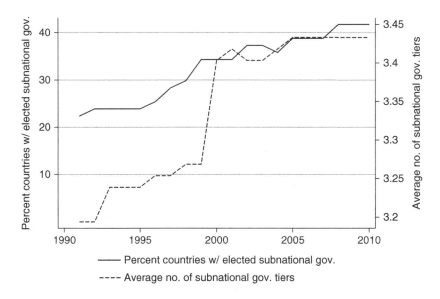

**Figure 3** Political and administrative decentralization in the developing world, 1991–2010

**Sources:** Authors' calculations. Underlying data are for sixty-seven developing countries from Bohlken (2016).

track the degree of administrative and political decentralization across sixty-seven developing countries over time. Both measures suggest an increase in decentralization, with the measure of political decentralization – the percent of countries wherein all subnational government tiers have elections – doubling from 20 percent in 1991 to 40 percent in 2010. As we detail later, we have reasons to believe that political decentralization in particular mediates the relationship between migration and nativism.

One example of the trend toward decentralization is India amending its Constitution in the early 1990s to mandate that the existing federal states all have village, city, and district level elected governments. Some authoritarian countries, notably China and Vietnam, implemented village level elections without opening up national participation. In cases of incomplete democratization or democratic reversals, such as Putin's Russia, the cycle of local and regional elections continues subject to central manipulation (Ross 2014). Importantly, Figure 3 shows that the use of subnational elections has been accompanied by greater and not less administrative decentralization. Administrative decentralization is measured by the average number of tiers of subnational government in developing countries. This metric of administrative decentralization has only increased along with the greater use of subnational elections.

Decentralization is also bound up with the issues of urban growth and rural-to-urban migration. Urban governments find themselves overseeing a mushrooming number of people. Suburbs influence the life of the city but may lie outside its political jurisdiction. These suburbs instead fall under purview of "rural" jurisdictions that are frequently designed with different legal powers and administrative capacities than urban authorities. In 2015, the United Nations found that almost half of less-developed countries were undertaking "decentralization of large urban centres to smaller urban, suburban or rural areas" in response to internal migration (DESA 2015: n.p.).

Finally, the number of countries that have one or more subnational ethnically defined jurisdictions has been increasing since the 1950s (Lacina 2017). Anderson (2014) notes twenty-seven countries that have at least one ethnofederal state or province where some ethnic group has special rights. Migrants from ethnically distinct parts of the same countries would be unable to obtain the same privileges on moving to these areas.

### 2.6.2 Decentralization Draws Lines for Nativism

Decentralization is not a necessary condition for controversy over internal migration. Sons-of-the-soil insurgency in southern Thailand, for example, has been intermittent for decades despite the absence of any elected subnational government there. Nonetheless, political decentralization increases the salience of sons-of-the-soil politics.[16] When smaller political jurisdictions are created, local ethnic divides are the likely fault lines for competition in the new jurisdictions (Posner 2005). Political scientists know, for example, that federal democracies tend to have more regionalist parties (Harmel and Robertson 1985).

Internal migrants only exist relative to some rhetorical or real subnational boundary. Political competition within subnational borders increases the number of subnational borders that could be the basis of an electorally convenient nativism. That is, a definition of nativism that allows a politician to define his or her constituents as sons-of-the-soil and label people who are not his or her voters as interlopers. For example, in Indonesia, "[i]f SoS [sons-of-the-soil] narratives are ubiquitous to local Indonesian politics, they are almost

---

[16] Ironically, some recommend decentralization as a solution to ethnic conflict between (rather than within) regions. Whether this works is disputed (Roeder 2009; Graham, Miller, and Strøm 2017).

completely absent from national politics" (Côté and Mitchell, 2016: 665). Côté and Mitchell point out that sons-of-the-soil narratives are a hard sell in national politics. The largest ethnic group in Indonesia, the Javanese, is only a plurality of the population and concentrated in less than a third of the country's provinces. By contrast, a majority of voters in a district or provincial election can be targeted with a sons-of-the-soil appeal.

Political decentralization exacerbates commitment problems that underlie sons-of-the-soil dynamics. As Fearon and Laitin (2011) note, internal migration has the potential to change subnational electorates even if the demography of the national electorate stays constant. If migrants can join the local electorate, migration poses a long-term threat to natives' political power. Governments should be able to stave off the nativist reaction to migration by catering to natives via redistribution or limiting migration. They have trouble, however, committing to such actions because rulers cannot tie the hands of their successors. Decentralization worsens this commitment problem because multiple governments have trouble working together, especially since they might be controlled by different political factions.

Finally, migration creates externalities between subnational jurisdictions. Migrant-sending areas may underinvest in policies that would discourage out-migration, such as securing land rights, or in mitigating natural disasters (United Nations 2014). The central government may be able to ameliorate that problem by transferring resources among units. If it does not do so, the interjurisdictional externalities reinforce the salience of local nativism.

The coming sections show that political decentralization increases the likelihood of sons-of-the-soil issues becoming an important part of politics. Locally responsive subnational governments can be expected to cater to non-migrants and regional ethnic majorities. Political decentralization strengthens the positive relationship between internal migration and the use of nativist appeals by local politicians, as well as the odds of regional governments enacting nativist policies.

### 2.6.3 Decentralization and Nativist Rioting

The relationship between decentralization, migration, and nativist rioting is likely to be ambiguous. Political decentralization boosts the salience of internal migration, but it also makes local governments more responsive to sons-of-the-soil concerns. If control over local affairs swings strongly toward the nativists, state repression of migrants is more likely than nonstate violence against migrants.

Consider, for example, the politics of ethnic homelands in Africa (Boone 2017). Neocustomary land rules give locals control over migration. When local conditions shift, migrants are "deported" to their own ethnic group's homeland. These deportations do not lead to sustained violence, however, because official support for deportation makes it impossible for settlers to resist and unnecessary for natives to rebel. For instance, local control of migration shaped conflict in KwaZulu-Natal, South Africa, in the early 1990s. In settlements around Durban, there were clashes between the African National Congress and the Inkatha Party and also between earlier and later arrivals to the settlements. Bekker and Louw (1994) describe a period of peace in the Tshelimnyama settlement. Tshelimnyama, unlike most of the informal settlements around Durban, had a well-established local governing committee. Bekker and Louw argue that "residents and community organisations perceived control over the entry of strangers to be directly linked to preventing violence" (p. 101). Specifically, local committees controlled in-migration, favoring the families of residents for admission. Then a political entrepreneur began selling sites without approval, and, when the committee could not stop the resulting influx, conflict between locals and migrants ensued. If decentralization aligns government power with native interests, effective use of that power in favor of locals may obviate nativist violence.

## 2.7 What to Expect from Internal Migration

Internal migration is booming. The next two sections show that in developing countries, greater numbers of internal migrants flowing into a jurisdiction increase the nonmigrant populations' receptivity to sons-of-the-soil appeals. Nativist politics becomes a larger force in the public sphere. Greater numbers of internal migrants increase the probability of the regional or national government implementing sons-of-the-soil policies such as affirmative action for natives, spending targeted at natives, and government discrimination against migrants. Violence by nonmigrants aimed at migrant expulsion and intimidation becomes more likely.

An important intermediate variable between migration and policy is the degree of political decentralization in a country. Under political decentralization, internal migration is even more likely to prompt nativist appeals by local politicians and nativist policies by regional governments. We also explore the relationship between decentralization, migration, and violence. We do not expect – and we do not find – a clear positive relationship between political decentralization and nativist rioting. Although decentralization increases the salience of anti-migrant politics, it also increases the probability that government policy will be pro-native. These pro-native policies sometimes prevent nonstate nativist violence even though strong anti-migrant sentiments prevail.

## 3 Nativist Parties and Policies

Subnational migration sets the stage for successful nativist political appeals. On the one hand, internal migrants are usually politically weak for several reasons, including because they are few in number, heterogeneous, and frequently unable to vote. On the other hand, natives increasingly see the need for protection from the stresses of migration, be it labor market competition, urban overcrowding, or some other malady. Entrepreneurial politicians rush in to fill that gap. In some cases, existing politicians and parties lead the charge on nativism. At other times, new leaders, parties, or factions surge to prominence by advocating for sons-of-the-soil measures.

This section shows the connection between migration and the growth of sons-of-the-soil parties and the amplifying effect of political decentralization on that relationship. Decentralization creates new, smaller political arenas in which nativism is likely to be a winning electoral strategy. We also examine the policy response to internal migration.

We begin by exploring how internal migration bolstered the fortunes of India's most famous nativist party, the Shiv Sena.

### 3.1 Shivaji's Army

The Shiv Sena (Shivaji's Army) was born in Mumbai (then Bombay) in western India. The party's namesake is the founder of the Maratha kingdom, Shivaji, who lived in the seventeenth century. The Sena argues for the right of Marathi speakers to preeminence in the land of Shivaji. The party periodically redefines which non-Maratha migrants are the foremost hindrance to Maratha ascendancy as the composition of migration shifts and the Sena's appeal spreads beyond Mumbai. The Sena is notorious for fomenting riots that polarize communities and mobilize the pro-Sena vote (Wilkinson 2004: 47–48).

With a population of over 18 million, Mumbai is India's largest city and is one of the largest in the world. Mumbai is a city of immigrants from other parts of Maharashtra, the state of which it is the capital, and also substantially from other parts of the country. In 1991, 21 percent of the city's population was from other Indian states. In 2001, migrants were 27 percent of the city's population. Because many men migrate into the city in search of work, the city has a particularly skewed sex ratio (approximately 850 females for every 1,000 males). Mumbai is exceedingly diverse in terms of religions, languages spoken, and states of origin. While 67 percent of the city's inhabitants are Hindu, 19 percent are Muslim, 5 percent are Buddhist, 4 percent are Jain, and 4 percent are Muslim. Marathi (spoken by 40 percent of the city's population) and Hindi are frequently spoken, and English is the city's lingua franca.

Mumbai is India's financial and commercial capital and generates approximately 7 percent of the country's gross domestic product (GDP). The city contributes 25 percent of India's industrial output, although this share has somewhat declined over time, especially after the textile sector collapsed in the 1980s. Because Mumbai is a port city, trade and allied services, including finance, are big employers. Like many large cities across the world, especially in poor, developing countries, Mumbai faces population-related stresses, including the underprovisioning of infrastructure (e.g., for drinking water, sanitation, and housing), education, and healthcare. Over 50 percent of the population lives in slums that occupy just 6 percent of the city's land (Verma 2011: 751). In addition to rapid population growth, Mumbai has a notable (above country average) surplus of men over women, which has been linked with violence (South, Trent, and Bose 2014).

Mumbai's politics is structured along the native-migrant cleavage. The Shiv Sena champions Marathi-speaking Maharashtrians, known as "Marathas."[17] A 2006 splinter party, the Maharashtra Navnirman Sena, draws support from the same population. Within Mumbai municipal politics, the Indian National Congress (INC), the Nationalist Congress Party (NCP), and the leftist parties have countered the Sena by being more pro-migrant and pro-minority. In state level elections, the INC and NCP draw substantial support from Marathas because anti-migrant Marathi nativism has historically been less salient in other parts of the state.

The Shiv Sena rose to power by helping organize disaffected middle-class Marathas who were laid off during Mumbai's deindustrialization since the 1970s. In 1971–2001, the city's industrial workers declined from 42 percent of the workforce to 29 percent, providing a fertile ground for political mobilization. In an illustration of the power of decentralization to create new identities for political mobilization, the Sena was also the unintended beneficiary of the successful movement to carve out a state for Marathi speakers – Maharashtra – from the erstwhile Bombay state. Gavaskar (2010) argues that the Shiv Sena was able to grow in the 1960s because the Maharashtra Congress Party, having won a state, did not insist on Marathi cultural prominence in Mumbai. The Shiv Sena rose to power mobilizing grievances specifically

---

[17] "Maratha" also refers to the Maratha caste, which is just one of many Marathi-speaking castes. The Shiv Sena is historically especially strong with Maratha caste Marathi-speakers.

against urban migrants. The initial objects of the Shiv Sena's ire were South Indian migrants. In the 1980s and 1990s, the party targeted Muslims, often claiming that they were migrants from other states or immigrants from Bangladesh. Even more recently, the Sena has targeted North Indians, particularly Biharis.

The Shiv Sena has dominated Mumbai's municipal government – the Brihanmumbai Municipal Corporation – since the mid-1980s. This has been a key resource for the party because the city's annual budget – at approximately $5 billion – is the largest in the country and is larger than the budgets of some of India's smaller states.

The Shiv Sena and allied parties have sought to address nativist sentiment by denying domestic migrants services and identification documents, frequently on the pretext that they are illegal aliens (Abbas 2016). The Sena has also sought to improve the employment prospects of natives via the promotion of Marathi and job quotas for locals. Such efforts have included making Marathi the official language of the municipal government, forbidding (legally and on the threat of vigilante violence) the production of government documents in Hindi and English, and for businesses, the compulsory installation of name boards in Marathi. In a related, largely symbolic move, the party renamed Bombay as Mumbai.[18]

The Shiv Sena has also agitated for reservations for Maharashtrians and specific subgroups of Maharashtrians. Other parties have had to incorporate some of the same goals into their platforms. In 2014, the Congress-led government of Maharashtra announced that 16 percent of government jobs and educational seats would be "reserved," or set aside, for Marathas. These "reservations" (as quotas are known in India) are in addition to existing reservations (which covered 52 percent of the population) for disadvantaged castes and tribes, almost all of which are Marathi-speaking.[19] The state government has also pressured private-sector firms to ensure that the bulk of their workforce is Maharashtrian (Verma 2011).

Among Maharashtrians across Maharashtra state, there has historically been a distinction between those in Mumbai for whom migration was highly salient and Maharashtrians elsewhere. Maratha nativism has become an increasingly powerful state level political force in part because migrant communities of Mumbai are spreading into suburban districts (Palshikar 2010). The next subsection shows quantitatively how successful the Sena has been in making inroads into areas of Maharashtra that are feeling new stress from internal migration.

---

[18] "Mumbai" is considered to be indigenous, although it is arguably just as invented as "Bombay."
[19] Subsequently, reservations for Marathas have been withdrawn due to the requirement – articulated by the Supreme Court – that reservations be capped at 50 percent.

### 3.1.1 Analyzing the Shiv Sena's Electoral Success

The Shiv Sena's signature issue in Mumbai politics is anti-migrant mobilization. This subsection probes whether the flow of out-of-state migrants to Maharashtra aided the Sena's rise. The fact that the Shiv Sena's core supporters are concentrated in migrant-receiving cities, particularly Mumbai, is consistent with the hypothesis that out-of-state migration helped the rise of the Sena. We do not mean to suggest that such in-migration mechanically translates into support for the Shiv Sena. Far from it. The Shiv Sena is purposive in ensuring the party profits from out-of-state-migration. As Weiner (1978) and Hansen (2001) have shown, the party mobilizes people through periodic anti-migrant campaigns, propaganda (frequently disseminated through its mouthpiece, the *Saamna*), general strikes or *bandhs*, vigilante violence, and even riots.

To systematically examine whether migration causes increased Shiv Sena support, we examine the party's performance in elections to Maharashtra's state legislature. These elections are held every four to five years (the exact period between elections varies slightly because the executive has some discretion over when elections are called) and occur in single-member constituencies (electoral districts) on a simple plurality or first-past-the-post basis. We measure the political response to migration within each administrative district, which is the level at which we observe migration. There are four to thirty-four constituencies in each administrative district, with an average of eleven constituencies. We employ three dependent variables: the proportion of constituencies in an administrative district in which a Shiv Sena candidate ran for office, the proportion of votes won by the Shiv Sena, and the proportion of constituencies won by the Shiv Sena. The presence of Shiv Sena candidates mostly reflects party strategy, whereas votes and winners are jointly determined by parties and voters. Our electoral data are for the five most recent state elections, starting in 1985.

Our key independent variable of interest is the log number of out-of-state domestic migrants, measured for the five years before each state election. The migration data that we employ are from the Census of India 1981, 1991, and 2001. The Census asks each person how long he or she has been resident in a place (<1 year, 1–4 years, 5–9 years, or 10–19 years or longer) and from which state he or she came. This implicitly defines a series of unequal time periods and in-migration in each of those periods.[20] We estimate annual rates of

---

[20] For example, in the 2001 Census, the number of people who reported being resident in a state for one to four years (and previously living elsewhere in India) was an estimate of that state's in-migration between 1997 and 1999. The number of people who reported being resident in the state for five to nine years was an estimate of in-migration between 1992 and 1996, and so on.

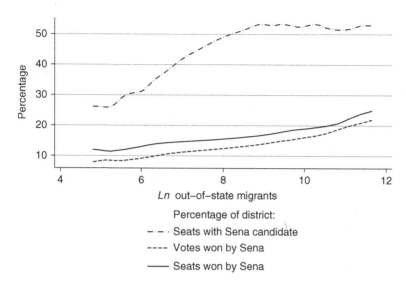

**Figure 4** The electoral performance of the Shiv Sena in Maharashtra state
elections and internal migration, 1985–2004

migration[21] and average them over the five years prior to each of Maharashtra's
elections.

In Figure 4, we explore the bivariate relationship between our measures of
the Shiv Sena's electoral performance and migration. Consistent with our
theory, migration is positively related to the proportion of constituencies with
Shiv Sena candidates, the Shiv Sena's vote share, and the proportion of constituencies where the Shiv Sena won office.

To explore the positive relationship between migration and the electoral
performance of the Shiv Sena suggested in Figure 4 rigorously, we turn to
regression. Model 1 of Table 4 (full results are in Appendix Table S2) reports
the bivariate relationship between migration and the percent of seats where the
Shiv Sena fielded a candidate. The two variables are positively related to
a statistically significant degree. In Model 2, we control for a variety of district
level factors that could affect both migration and the dependent variables.
We control for income per capita because high incomes might attract migrants
and increase right-wing party support. We also control for population and
urbanization because these might proxy for resource competition, which
would deter migrants and increase right-wing voting. Further, we draw on the
sons-of-the-soil literature to control for school enrollment rates and the

---

[21] For example, the annual migration rate for 1992 is calculated as the number of migrants that
entered the state between 1992 and 1996 divided by 5.

**Table 4** Multivariate Analysis of the Electoral Performance of the Shiv Sena in Maharashtra State Elections and Internal Migration, 1985–2004

| | *Ln* % seats with Sena candidate | | | | *Ln* % Sena vote | *Ln* % Sena seats |
| | OLS | OLS | 2SLS | | 2SLS | 2SLS |
| | Model 1 | Model 2 | Model 3 | | Model 4 | Model 5 |
| | | | First stage | Second stage | Second stage | Second stage |
|---|---|---|---|---|---|---|
| *Ln* out-of-state migrants | 0.37*** | 0.67** | | 5.9*** | 4.0*** | 1.7** |
| | (0.10) | (0.25) | | (0.91) | (0.67) | (0.79) |
| Abnormal monsoon instrument | | | 1.6*** | | | |
| | | | (0.27) | | | |
| District dummies | Y | Y | Y | Y | Y | Y |
| Controls | N | Y | Y | Y | Y | Y |
| Observations | 129 | 129 | 129 | 129 | 129 | 129 |
| Adjusted $R^2$ | 0.08 | 0.35 | | | | |
| First-stage *F*-statistic | | | 34 | | | |
| Second-stage *F*-statistic | | | | 14 | 9 | 1 |

**Note:** Control variables, measured for the host district, are abnormal monsoon rainfall, land degradation, income per capita, population, urbanization, male children's school enrollment rates, the share of the native male population aged fifteen to nineteen years, and district fixed effects. Standard errors, clustered by district, are in parentheses (OLS = ordinary least squares; 2SLS = two-stage least squares). *$p < 0.1$; **$p < 0.05$; ***$p < 0.01$.

proportion of people aged fifteen to nineteen years because these might be correlated with violence and migration. We include two controls related to our instrumentation strategy, which is discussed further later. These are abnormal monsoons and degraded lands. Lastly, we include district fixed effects, which control for district-specific, time-invariant factors (such as underlying receptivity to migrants) that might affect our independent and dependent variables. Controlling for these factors, the estimated partial correlation between migration and the percent of seats with a Sena candidate is larger than before.

### 3.1.2 A Natural Experiment to Determine Causality

Efforts to examine the effects of migration on politics face three related problems. First, frequently unobservable factors such as psychological stress could explain both anti-migrant politics and where migrants go. Second, the direction of causality could be reversed: politics likely affects patterns of migration. And third, migration could be mismeasured. These "endogeneity" problems interfere with estimating the causal relationship between migration and the electoral performance of the Shiv Sena. In particular, if migrants stay away from places that vote for the Shiv Sena, standard OLS estimates of the effect of migration on the Shiv Sena vote would be attenuated.

To ensure that the estimated effects of migration on politics are indeed causal, we turn to a "natural experiment" due to natural disaster–induced migration. Drawing on previous work (Bhavnani and Lacina 2015), we instrument for migration into Maharashtra's districts with a population- and distance-weighted measure of abnormal rainfall in migrant-sending states. Excess and deficient monsoons induce migration through economic hardship.[22] Landholders and rural laborers are pushed into migration by agricultural downturns (Kochar 1999; Rose 2001). The monsoon season, which accounts for 75 percent of India's annual rainfall, also routinely displaces millions of people due to flooding (Mall et al. 2006). The EM-DAT (2011) data set reports that the annual average of flood-affected people in India between 1961 and 2011 was 6 million, whereas a 1991 study estimated that up to 30 million Indians were displaced annually by flooding.[23]

Inadequate and/or excess rainfall has been used as an instrument for income in India and elsewhere.[24] Predicting migration requires a slightly different

---

[22] Cole, Healy, and Werker (2012); Jacoby and Skoufias (1997); Kumar (2011); Mendelsohn, Dinar, and Sanghi (2001); Jayachandra (2006).

[23] Cited in Lama (2000: 25).

[24] For India, see Bohlken and Sergenti (2010) and Kapur, Gawande, and Satyanath (2012). For other settings, see Mehlum, Miguel, and Torvik (2006); Miguel, Satyanath, and Sergenti (2004); Bergholt and Lujala (2012); Brückner and Ciccone (2011).

strategy. We observe monsoons in migrant-sending areas in order to predict migration to a host area. We measure rainfall outside the district for which we are predicting migration and use these shocks to the supply of migrants to instrument for population inflows. We control for weather in the migrant-receiving area and account for environmental and economic spillovers between India's regions.

Our instrument is based on abnormal monsoon rainfall, defined by the Indian Ministry of Agriculture as 20 percent below or above average rainfall in the monsoon season. Inspired by the gravity model of trade (Frankel and Romer 1999), we code a dummy variable for states with excess or deficient monsoon rainfall in a year[25] and multiply that term by the population of the affected state; then we divide by the distance between the affected state and the potential host district in Maharashtra. The instrument for an individual district (indexed by $i$) is the sum of these terms across Indian states (indexed by $j$) other than Maharashtra. The instrument for district $i$ is

$$Ln\left(\sum_j \frac{\text{abnormal rainfall}_j \times \text{population}_j}{\text{distance}_{ij}}\right)$$

Figure 5 is a scatterplot of the instrument and our migration data (both have been "partialed out" using controls) with a line of best fit. The monsoon instrument is positively correlated ($\rho = 0.4$) with average annual migration into districts.

Migrants select destinations with more criteria than distance in mind. A more exhaustive predictor of migration would include the pull factors, other than physical proximity, that might bring people to one Indian state over another. For our purposes, however, we need to predict migration to a particular district with an instrument that does not affect local politics via channels other than migration. For example, migrants may favor destinations that have had high previous levels of migration or choose destinations that are culturally similar to their place of origin. In India, language differences are likely to shape migration. However, incorporating historical migration or language affinities into our predictor of migration would be a problematic research design. These cultural factors are related to our dependent variables, which measure the success of the ethnic chauvinist Shiv Sena.

We have taken care to select an instrument for migration that does not include host district characteristics. However, there is still a possibility that the weather disasters we chart could influence politics in Maharashtra via other pathways.

---

[25] Using data from Parthasarathy, Munot, and Kothawale (1994); Parthasarathy (2001); and Parthasarathy, Munot, and Kothawale (1995), compiled by Indiastat (2000).

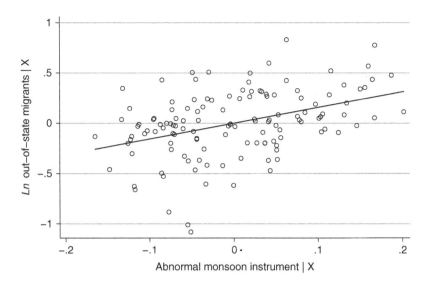

**Figure 5** Scatterplot of internal migration into Maharashtra's districts and abnormal monsoon instrument, 1985–2004, with a line of best fit

**Note:** Control variables ($X$), measured for the host district, are abnormal monsoon rainfall, land degradation, income per capita, population, urbanization, male children's school enrollment rates, the share of the native male population aged fifteen to nineteen years, and district fixed effects.

First, as noted earlier, we obviously need to control for receiving districts' own monsoon conditions. Second, adverse monsoons in other states may have environmental spillovers. Heavy monsoons may cause flooding or water erosion in Maharashtra's districts, whereas drought may lead to downstream wind erosion. In the regressions that follow, we control for land degradation, including flooding and wind erosion, in the host district. Third, an adverse monsoon in one state may have economic spillovers for neighbors. In order to control for this possibility, we include as a control host district per capita income.

As Model 3 of Table 4 suggests, our abnormal rainfall instrument is positively and significantly related to migration, our endogenous variable. Importantly, the first-stage $F$-statistic is well above 10, which means that the instrument is strong. The second stage estimates the effect of migration on the percent of seats that the Shiv Sena runs in. This effect is large and statistically significant: a 10 percent increase in migration causes a 59 percent increase in the percent of seats that the Shiv Sena ran in, from a mean of 46 to 73 percent.

In Models 4 and 5 of Table 4, we employ two-stage least squares (2SLS) to estimate the effects of migration on our two other dependent variables. Model 4 suggests that a 10 percent increase in migration causes a 40 percent increase in the percent of votes received by the Shiv Sena (from a mean of 13 to 18 percent), whereas Model 5 suggests that the same increase in migration causes a 17 percent increase in the percent of seats won by the party (from a mean of 16 to 19 percent). Both results are substantively and statistically significant.

We now have strong causal evidence, due to a disaster-induced natural experiment, that migration helped cause the rise of the archetypal nativist party – the Shiv Sena – in the Indian state of Maharashtra. Do these findings extend elsewhere?

## 3.2 Migration and Latin American Indigenous Parties

There is no ready indicator of how successful nativist politicians are in one country compared with another. Even setting aside countries without political parties or with strictly personalist parties, a general definition of sons-of-the-soil organizations is a problem. For example, in India, most political parties support nativist policies, even if they were not founded for the purpose of pursuing those policies. In any country where ethnic parties are the norm, distinguishing nativism is difficult. Most political parties in Sub-Saharan Africa are thought to be ethnic parties, and the majority of those ethnic groups consider themselves indigenous. A broad definition of sons-of-the-soil parties would capture almost all parties in Africa. A very narrow definition – for example, coding only parties that propose restrictions on migration as sons-of-the-soil – would miss de facto nativism.

Our solution to these definitional problems is inspired by Rice and Van Cott's (2006) study of indigenous parties in South America. In the 1990s, the combination of political liberalization and economic downturn destroyed major political parties in many Latin American countries. "Amid this widespread party system decomposition ... electorally viable political parties organized around indigenous identity" (Rice and Van Cott 2006: 710) emerged in several countries. Importantly for research purposes, Latin American indigenous parties are a well-defined category, delineated by regional experts interested in research questions distinct from ours.

Latin American indigenous parties are not typically described as sons-of-the-soil parties by international media. Internal migration is a key grievance for many of them nonetheless. The issues that recur most commonly across indigenous parties are demands for land titling and territorial autonomy, measures that address the incursion into indigenous areas by the state, commercial interests, and settlers or *colonos* ("colonists").

Indigenous Americans have a clear historical claim to being the sons-of-the-soil. Yet "indigenous" is an umbrella term for many cultures and languages in a plurinational project (Jackson and Warren 2005; Madrid 2005). Many people who self-identify as indigenous have some nonindigenous ancestors or speak only Spanish. Indigenous rights have also been extended in some cases to rural blacks (Plant 2002). Yet, and as we show later, the imprecise nature of "indigenous" identity has not been a barrier to gaining social and political currency.

Indigenous identity in the Americas does differ in two important respects from, for example, Maharashtrian identity in Maharashtra. First, indigenous Americans are in the numerical minority in most countries. Second and not coincidentally, Latin American governments have historically been hostile to indigenous interests and indigenous identity. In India, the state typically sides with the sons-of-the-soil. Military and police violence is generally committed on behalf of locals and against migrants. In Latin America, the pattern has instead been governments that support nonindigenous populations and aggressively promote economic expansion and population settlement in indigenous areas. Indigenous populations have borne the brunt of both state violence and state-abetted settler violence for centuries.

Indigenous politics obviously relates to the centuries-long confrontation between native and settler America. Does more recent domestic migration play any role in the success of Latin American indigenous parties at the end of the twentieth century? To answer this question, we build on Rice and Van Cott's comparison of the growth of indigenous parties in South America between the early 1990s – when indigenous parties were trivial or nonexistent – and elections in the 2000s. We analyze Ecuador, Peru, Colombia, Venezuela, and Bolivia and add two Central American cases, Nicaragua and Guatemala. By limiting our geographic and temporal context, we can define sons-of-the-soil politics in a consistent manner across our cases.

### 3.2.1 American Sons-of-the-Soil

Starting in the 1990s, indigenous political appeals found unprecedented success in Latin America. In Colombia, Ecuador, Nicaragua, Panama, and Venezuela, constitutions adopted in the 1990s included autonomous indigenous jurisdictions (Van Cott 2001). In 2002, the indigenous peoples' party, Pachakutik Movement of Plurinational Unity, was part of the winning presidential coalition in Ecuador. In 2006, Evo Morales became the first indigenous president of Bolivia.

In foreign media and nongovernmental organization (NGO) accounts, indigenous parties are described as a backlash against neoliberal economic policies, the International Monetary Fund (IMF) and World Bank, multinational agribusiness, and resource extraction (Jackson and Warren 2005). There are good strategic reasons for indigenous politicians to emphasize their environmentalism and critiques of neoliberalism. Economic nationalism and nonstrident ethnic appeals have enabled some indigenous parties to win substantial numbers of nonindigenous votes (Madrid 2005; Van Cott 2003). Also, the audience for indigenous appeals is partly global (Hvalkof 2000; McSweeney and Jokisch 2007). Indigenous parties can be helped by "an increasingly powerful trans-national indigenous movement, and by funding and support from multilateral institutions such as the Inter-American Development Bank (IDB) and the World Bank, as well as international NGOs" (Hooker 2005: 296). These partnerships are facilitated by endorsing causes such as conservation and population-centric development.

The policies endorsed by Latin American indigenous parties are profoundly concerned with internal migration. The oldest and most common theme for indigenous political parties is the demand for official titling of indigenous land and property. "Territory – gaining land rights – continues to be the prime goal of indigenous organizations" (Jackson and Warren 2005: 566). Titling programs can be conducted on behalf of individuals, communities, or both. The roots of indigenous mobilization in Ecuador, for example, are grassroots campaigns for land titling starting in 1969 (Perreault 2003). In 1992, a pro-land titling march to Quito catalyzed the national turn toward indigenous politics. Migration, in turn, was behind the demand for land titles.

> The principal organizers were the Organización de Pueblos Indígenas de Pastaza [Organization of Indigenous Peoples of Pastaza (OPIP)] . . . At the time of the march it claimed a constituency of 148 Quichua, Achuar, and Shiwiar communities, numbering approximately 20,000 people. Their mobilization was the culmination of a 14-year struggle in defense of ancestral lands. Since the mid-1960s, indigenous lowlanders east of the Andes had contended with the incursions of increasing numbers of highland and coastal homesteaders in search of a better life. (Sawyer 1997: 68)

The Tawahka in Honduras mobilized a political federation in response to settler invasions starting in 1986 (McSweeney and Jokisch 2007). Indigenous mobilization in Colombia began in the Cauca region with a movement to repossess coffee-growing land held by nonindigenous farmers (Ramos 2002). The fight for land titling continues as a struggle to enforce earlier titling programs (Stocks 2005). For example, even after Costa Rica's Salitre Indigenous Reserve was created, nonindigenous settlers were able to occupy 60 percent of the territory by squatting or illegally purchasing land. Indigenous mobilization aims to remove nonlocals who arrived after 1977 (McPhaul 2015). In this case, police and settlers have teamed up to attack indigenous mobilization and continue the land grabs.

A second goal of most indigenous political parties is territorial autonomy. The new political parties attempt to consolidate zones of indigenous control.

> Indigenous peoples are increasingly demanding that the state recognize territorial boundaries (even, or particularly, where they cut across municipal or provincial boundaries) in which social relations are regulated by indigenous authority systems and customary law. In other words, they are arguing that a differentiated citizenship should coincide with differentiated administrative boundaries. (Yashar 1999: 93)

Thus the project of indigenous parties includes reverse engineering ethnic jurisdictions such as the ones common in Africa and South Asia. In this cause, indigenous political parties have been aided by the trend toward decentralization in Latin America during the 1990s (Van Cott 2001).

An impetus for autonomy demands is encroaching development: agribusiness, mining and timber concessions, and settlers (Tock 2011; Cultural Survival 2012). Territorial autonomy is a means to ensure that development happens on terms favorable to locals. For example, in Ecuador's Illiniza Ecological Reserve, the indigenous community of Quilotoa has sought to block outside artists and entrepreneurs from participating in the growing tourist economy (Colloredo-Mansfeld et al. 2018). Indigenous rejection of state-led development or international business cannot be separated from anxiety about migration. Agribusiness and mineral extraction not only bring an outside workforce, but they also build infrastructure that allows migration to indigenous areas to surge. A major milestone in indigenous mobilization in Bolivia was the 1990 backlash against the opening of the Chiman Forest Reserve to "timber concessions, while unemployed miners and landless peasants poured into the Amazon seeking livelihoods in ranching and coca production" (Brysk and Wise 1997: 89).

The role of migration in indigenous politics is particularly obvious when migration brings the newly created zones of indigenous territorial autonomy into conflict with settlers who are also indigenous (McPhaul 2015; Brysk and Wise 1997; Sawyer, 1997). In Bolivia, Evo Morales' government introduced a constitution that grants indigenous communities the right to manage natural resources in their territories. However, the Morales government is politically aligned with highland indigenous communities and has supported upland colonists against the lowland indigenous.

> Highland peasants arrive as indigenous citizens to occupy land that is unused
> or underused in the relatively sparsely populated eastern lowlands; unused,
> that is, from the perspective of the colonists; not exactly unused from the
> perspective of the equally indigenous people who live there. (Canessa 2014:
> 163)

In 2011, the government overruled local indigenous groups' objections to road building in the autonomous Territorio Indígena Parque Nacional Isiboro Securé (Canessa 2014). The seeming paradox of the Morales government violating indigenous territorial autonomy is resolved by noting that in the conflict over Bolivian internal migration, the Morales government is aligned with the sons-of-the-soil in the highlands but with the settlers in the lowlands.

In the everyday lives of indigenous communities, the pressures of the globalizing economy are embodied by internal migration. As the next subsection shows, indigenous political parties have been especially successful in areas where economic foment brought the most significant population inflows.

### 3.2.2 Analyzing Indigenous Party Emergence

This subsection analyzes the increase in indigenous party vote share during national elections in Bolivia, Colombia, Ecuador, Guatemala, Nicaragua, Peru, and Venezuela (Table 5). The units of analysis are first-level administrative jurisdictions – e.g., departments in Guatemala – with indigenous populations. In these 124 areas, we observe the change in indigenous party vote share between an initial set of elections held around 1990 and a second wave of elections held between 2002 and 2011. Table 5 notes the specific election dates by country. The elections were chosen for each country so that they bracket the available data on domestic migration. The data on internal migration are from

**Table 5** Cases Used in the Analysis of Latin American Indigenous Parties

| Country | Election$_{t=0}$ | Election$_{t=1}$ | Migration data collection |
|---------|---------|---------|---------|
| Bolivia | 1989 | 2002 | 1996–2001 |
| Colombia | 1994 | 2002 | 2000–5 |
| Ecuador | 1990 | 2002 | 1996–2001 |
| Guatemala | 1990 | 2007 | 1996–2002 |
| Nicaragua | 1990 | 2001 | 2000–5 |
| Peru | 1990 | 2011 | 2002–7 |
| Venezuela | 1988 | 2010 | 2006–11 |

the IMAGE database introduced earlier. Our analysis relates the change in indigenous party vote share between the 1990s and 2000s to internal migration in the intervening period. By happy accident, the IMAGE data are from the interval during which indigenous parties were becoming an important electoral force in Latin America. In many countries, such as Malaysia, the growth of sons-of-the-soil parties was well underway by the time the IMAGE data were being collected.

Table 6 reports OLS regressions of the log change in the percent of the vote won by indigenous parties (full results are in Appendix Table S3). All the models use country fixed effects to capture national level factors that influence whether indigenous parties are likely to find any purchase (Rice and Van Cott 2006). The population and population density of each administrative unit capture the pull of urban areas and the stress of resource competition. The regressions also control for the indigenous population share – any backlash against migration is presumably increasing in this variable[26] – and income per capita, which likely draws in migrants and assuages anti-migrant sentiments. All controls are measured at the time of the first election in our data.

Model 1, which uses the control set described earlier, estimates that a 10 percent increase in migrant inflows translated to indigenous parties winning 1.3 percent more of the vote in later elections. Model 2 adds controls based on Rice and Van Cott's analysis of indigenous party vote share: the percentage of people under the poverty line and the share of the vote captured by left-wing parties in early 1990s elections, plus district magnitudes in the later wave of elections. Adding these factors to the analysis, Model 2 estimates a similarly sized and statistically significant correlation between in-migration and support for indigenous parties.

### 3.2.3 A Role for Political Decentralization

Van Cott (2003) argues that indigenous parties owe some of their recent success to greater political decentralization in Latin America. Municipal and provincial elections helped indigenous parties in Bolivia and Ecuador gain a foothold and then extend their participation into national elections. Colombia has indigenous parties despite a very small indigenous population in part because constitutional reforms in 1991 created indigenous *resguardos*, similar to municipalities.

This account is consistent with our argument that political decentralization aids sons-of-the-soil political appeals by defining new arenas for political

---

[26] The initial ethnic composition of a district is captured by district fixed effects in the Shiv Sena analysis earlier.

**Table 6** Multivariate OLS Analysis of the Log Change in the Vote Percent of Latin American Indigenous Parties and Internal Migration

|  | Model 1 | Model 2 | Model 3 |
|---|---|---|---|
| *Ln* migrants | 0.13** | 0.12* |  |
|  | (0.039) | (0.043) |  |
| *Ln* migrants × political decentralization |  |  | 0.14* |
|  |  |  | (0.068) |
| *Ln* migrants × no political decentralization |  |  | −0.11 |
|  |  |  | (0.17) |
| Country dummies | Y | Y | Y |
| Controls | Y | Y | Y |
| Additional controls | N | Y | Y |
| Observations | 124 | 124 | 124 |
| Adjusted $R^2$ | 0.87 | 0.87 | 0.87 |

**Note:** Control variables in all models are indigenous population share, PPP-adjusted GDP per capita, logged population, and logged urban population share among nonmigrants. The additional controls are poverty, initial vote share of left parties, and district magnitude in the second observed election. Standard errors, clustered by country, in parentheses. $*p < 0.1$; $**p < 0.05$; $***p < 0.01$.

competition and by giving politicians the incentives and ability to define their voters as natives and appeal to nativism. What does the quantitative evidence from Latin America suggest? To examine this question, we disaggregate the variable for internal migration into two terms so that the relationship between migration and indigenous party vote share is estimated separately for decentralized and not decentralized countries. We emphasize that since decentralization is not exogenously assigned, we are not making causal claims about the effects of decentralization but are instead simply examining how the migration-voting relationship varies in country-years with and without decentralization. We note which countries had elected executives in subnational administrative units at the time of the first elections in our data.[27] Some countries, including Bolivia and Ecuador, pursued decentralization later in part because of pressure from indigenous mobilization.

---

[27] Our decentralization measure is based on Cruz, Keefer, and Scartascini (2016) and Beck et al. (2001), with missing data filled in using US Department of the Army (2003), Bohlken (2016), and The Hunger Project (2014).

The first new variable in Model 3 (Table 6) is labeled "*Ln* migrants × political decentralization." It measures population inflows for countries with political decentralization in place at the beginning of our period of study. This variable is zero for countries where political decentralization was not already in place in the early 1990s. The second new variable in Model 3 is labeled "*Ln* migrants × no political decentralization." This variable records migrant inflows for politically centralized countries and is zero for all other countries.[28]

The positive relationship between migration and indigenous party vote share is larger in relatively decentralized places than elsewhere. In politically decentralized countries, a 10 percent increase in migration is associated with indigenous parties receiving 1.4 percent more of the vote in national elections. The correlation between migration and indigenous party vote share is indeterminate in countries without political decentralization.[29] These results are consistent with an amplifying role of political decentralization in the success of sons-of-the-soil politicians.

The next subsection is a more ambitious investigation of the role of political decentralization in the politics of domestic migration. We look at India's staggered rollout of local elections and its implications for government treatment of migrants. This analysis is more ambitious in two regards. First, we seek to make stronger causal claims about the effects of decentralization using a difference-in-difference estimator. And second, our dependent variable is not a measure of the rise of nativist politicians or parties, or even the enactment of anti-migrant policies, but rather a measure of plausibly discriminatory government behavior.

## 3.3 Panchayati Raj and Migrants

Political decentralization paves the way for sons-of-the-soil politicians and policies. India's staggered rollout of elected substate governments shows that as localities became more accountable to local people, bureaucrats become more discriminatory toward migrants from other states.

India is a federal country with elected state governments. States are loosely based on ethnic regions (Lacina 2014). In the past, most states did not have or had weak elected bodies at the district, village, or municipal levels. In the early 1990s, the center pushed the states to add lower levels of elected government. India's 73rd Constitutional Amendment was ratified and

---

[28] The setup of Model 3 is equivalent to having a variable for migration, a variable for political decentralization, and an interaction of the two. The variable for political decentralization would drop out of the model due to country fixed effects. The resulting coefficients and standard errors could be rearranged to obtain the results in Table 6.

[29] The difference between the two coefficients is not statistically significant.

became law in 1993.[30] "This Act required each state to set up a three-tier system of local government, comprising village, intermediate and district level governance bodies, collectively known as the Panchayati Raj" (Iyer et al. 2012: 169). These new local bodies are entirely elected and supervise local services, such as roads, sanitation, and education.[31] Before Panchayati Raj, the bureaucracies implementing these services were answerable to the state government. The Panchayati Raj is an additional local principal for these administrators.

Madhya Pradesh, Punjab, and Tripura held panchayat elections the year after the 73rd Amendment passed (Alok 2014). Other states were laggards. Arunachal Pradesh only held panchayat elections in 2003. Jharkhand's inaugural panchayat elections were in 2010.

Iyer et al. (2012) argues that variation in the timing of the implementation of the Panchayati Raj reflects previously established state election calendars, lawsuits, and low state capacity. "For instance, elections in Bihar were delayed due to a lawsuit challenging the proposed reservation for Other Backward Castes (OBCs) that had not been explicitly mandated by the constitutional amendment" (Iyer et al. 2012: 171). These factors have no obvious relationship to the politics of migration. As we argue later, this factor is critical for our empirical strategy to examine the effects of decentralization on anti-migrant discrimination. We turn to describing our dependent variable next.

### 3.3.1 Government Employment in India

Did decentralization result in more local government discrimination against migrants?[32] To answer this question, we look at government employment. In 2012, approximately 17 million Indians worked in government or government-run businesses and industries, accounting for 60 percent of formal employment (MOSPI 2012: Table 32.1). Only approximately six million government workers were employed by the center. Nine million were state government employees, and two million were local government employees. The eleven million people in the state and local categories carry out work that could be subject to panchayat oversight. Unlike central government civil servants, state and local workers cannot be transferred between states.

---

[30] The law did not apply to Meghalaya, Mizoram, and Nagaland, which have alternative, older provisions for local governance in the Constitution. These three states and the union territories are not included in our analysis, with the exception of the capital territory of Delhi.

[31] The 73rd Amendment specifies twenty-nine functions that may be devolved to the panchayats at the discretion of the states.

[32] On state level discrimination in India, see Lacina (2017).

There are high barriers to migrants accessing state and local government employment. Since 1968, state and local governments are required to fill some positions through local employment exchanges.[33] India's Employment Exchanges Act has been in place since 1959. It provides for a network of 969 exchanges, at least one in every state except Sikkim. The state (or union territory) governments administer the exchanges (MOSPI 2012: 90). In 2012, 9.7 million Indians were newly registered on an employment exchange, contributing to a total of 45 million active registrations (MOSPI 2012: Table 32.12).

The employment exchanges require local residency.

> Under the rules of the employment exchanges, only residents of a district can register at local exchanges. An exception is made for graduates and other technically trained people who can apply to exchanges wherever they are located *within the same state.* (Weiner 1978: 341, original emphasis)

Thus, to legally participate in the exchange, a migrant must show residency, which requires the cooperation of local bureaucrats.[34] Bureaucrats stonewall migrants so often that some NGOs serving migrants issue identity cards and set up their own employment exchanges (Deshingkar and Farrington 2009). If decentralization has increased the sensitivity of local bureaucrats to sons-of-the-soil pressure, they would be more likely to deny migrants a spot on the employment exchange. Thus political decentralization is likely to curb migrant government employment by limiting migrant access to employment exchanges and through discrimination at the hiring stage.

### 3.3.2 Decentralization and Discrimination

To examine how patterns of government employment respond to decentraliza-tion, we use micro data from three rounds of India's national employment survey, from 1983, 1987, and 1999. Our dependent variable is a dummy for government employment, observed for close to a million respondents aged eighteen to sixty-five. In our data, 2.6 percent of respondents were employed by the government (the government employment rate was 2.5 percent for natives and 4.3 percent for migrants; 1.5 percent of survey respondents in the eighteen to sixty-five age range reported that they had migrated between India's states within the last five years). We use the exogenous timing of decentralization in a difference-in-differences analysis to examine the effects of decentralization on government employment. To examine whether decentralization caused governments to favor

---

[33] In the same announcement, the central government stated that private firms are encouraged to do the same. State governments have a history of pressuring private firms to use the exchanges (Weiner 1978).

[34] This discretion cuts two ways. Nonresidents can bribe their way onto exchanges (Weiner 1978).

locals over migrants, we further examine whether the decentralization "treatment" had heterogeneous effects on migrants versus natives.

Table 7 presents the difference-in-differences analysis. The unit of analysis in these regressions is an individual survey respondent, and the dependent variable is a dummy for government employment. All the regressions control for individuals' age, sex, education level, and whether they lived in an urban area, all of which could affect government employment. In Models 1 and 3, we include dummy variables for each state and year, and standard errors are clustered by state. These regressions therefore control for slow-moving or time-invariant factors that influenced the timing of Panchayati Raj, such as state election calendars. In Models 2 and 4, we include dummies for each state-year, and standard errors are clustered at this level. These regressions therefore control for an even more extensive control set: all state-year-invariant factors. The decentralization dummy records whether a respondent's state had introduced Panchayati Raj by the time the respondent was answering the survey. We therefore compare people in the same state before and after Panchayati Raj. The variable "Years decentralized" records the number of years (zero to six) between the first Panchayati Raj elections in a state and when a respondent there was surveyed.

Our expectation is that decentralization increased the disparity in government employment between migrants and nonmigrants. Each regression includes an interaction term for migration (a characteristic of the respondent) and decentralization (a characteristic of the state). A negative coefficient on this variable implies that migrants are more disadvantaged relative to natives under decentralization.

In Model 1, the difference-in-difference analysis suggests that migrants are 1.6 percentage points less likely to be employed by the government than natives when the state is politically decentralized. This difference is statistically significant at the 5 percent level. Since the mean government employment rate for migrants is 4.3 percent, this represents a 38 percent reduction in the rate of government employment.

To see this, consider that absent decentralization, migrants have a slightly higher rate of public employment (0.7 percentage points more) than nonmigrants, although the difference is statistically insignificant. The sample here is large enough that it may be picking up national civil servants, who are traditionally posted outside their home territory (Bhavnani and Lee 2018). The difference in rates of government employment between migrants and nonmigrants is larger in states with Panchayati Raj, about 0.9 percentage points.[35] This gap is statistically significant at the 90 percent confidence

---

[35] The 0.9 percentage points is the difference between the coefficients on Migrant × political decentralization and the uninteracted migrant term.

**Table 7** Difference-in-Difference OLS Analysis of the Effects of
Decentralization on Government Employment in India, 1983–1999

|  | Model 1 | Model 2 | Model 3 | Model 4 |
|---|---|---|---|---|
| Migrant × political decentralization | −0.016** (0.0073) | −0.015** (0.0061) |  |  |
| Migrant × years decentralized |  |  | −0.0030** (0.0013) | −0.0028** (0.0012) |
| Out-of-state migrant | 0.0074 (0.0054) | 0.0068 (0.0048) | 0.0069 (0.0052) | 0.0064 (0.0047) |
| Political decentralization | −0.0011 (0.0020) |  |  |  |
| Years decentralized |  |  | 0.00011 (0.00036) |  |
| State dummies | Y | N | Y | N |
| Year dummies | Y | N | Y | N |
| State-year dummies | N | Y | N | Y |
| Controls | Y | Y | Y | Y |
| Observations | 965,325 | 965,325 | 965,325 | 965,325 |
| Adjusted $R^2$ | 0.06 | 0.06 | 0.06 | 0.06 |

Note: Control variables are sex, age, residence in an urban area, and education level. Standard errors, clustered by state (Models 1 and 2) or state-year (Models 3 and 4), in parentheses. $*p < 0.1$; $**p < 0.05$; $***p < 0.01$.

level. The difference-in-differences comparison is the gap between migrants and nonmigrants in states with Panchayati Raj (−0.9 percentage points) versus states without (+0.7 percentage points). We can reject the null hypothesis of no difference-in-differences at the 95 percent confidence level. This result is essentially unchanged with the addition of more demanding state-year fixed effects (Model 2). Government employment tilted against migrants after Panchayati Raj was introduced.

Models 3 and 4 estimate the growing disparity between migrants and non-migrants as decentralization takes effect. In Model 3, we use state and year fixed effects; Model 4 employs more demanding state-year fixed effects. In these models, we replace the interaction of the migrant and decentralization dummies with the interaction of a migrant dummy and the years since decentralization. Consistent with the previous two models, migrants are less likely to be employed as decentralization takes effect.

To see how the government employment of migrants changes with decentralization, consider Figure 6. The $y$-axis of this figure plots the predicted gap between the government employment rate among migrants versus nonmigrants. The $x$-axis is years of Panchayati Raj. Zero years is a state without decentralization. As in Models 1 and 2, without decentralization, migrants had approximately 0.6 percentage point higher rates of government employment, and this difference is statistically insignificant. Models 3 and 4 estimate that by three years after Panchayati Raj took effect, government employment shifted to slightly favor natives. After six years, the estimated rate of government employment among migrants was 1 percentage point behind natives' rate. Note the small coefficient on the uninteracted variable for years of decentralization in Model 3. It implies that the shift in favor of natives did not result from robust expansion of the total number of government employees. Instead, government hiring shifted in favor of natives without expanding much overall.

It is notoriously difficult to pinpoint the effects of institutional changes such as decentralization. These institutions rarely change, and when they do, the motives for the change are often intertwined with political outcomes observers would like to gauge. The staggered rollout of India's elected local governments is a unique window onto how decentralization shifts power in favor of the sons-of-the-soil. State and local government hiring in India is designed to favor local residents. As Panchayati Raj has been rolled out, a bias in government hiring favoring long-time residents has emerged.

## 3.4 Conclusions

Internal migration leads to demands for sons-of-the-soil protections from natives in migrant-receiving regions. This surge in demand is symbiotic with greater influence for politicians making nativist appeals. Political decentralization increases the success of sons-of-the-soil politicians and the probability of sons-of-the-soil policies being implemented. Section 4 turns to a particularly severe form of nativist politicking – rioting.

## 4 Migration and Sons-of-the-Soil Riots

Political violence is an important driver of migration. The UN High Commissioner for Refugees (Birkeland, Jennings, and Rushing 2012) estimates that in 2011 there were over 25 million internally displaced persons (IDPs) and another 15 million international refugees. Many of these people have been forced to move by large-scale violence. Scholars believe that population movements can also feed political violence. Refugee encampments

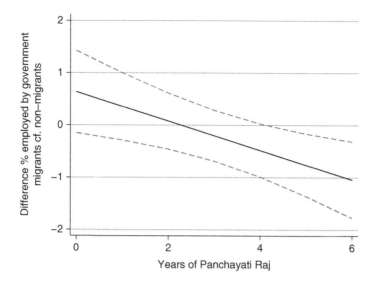

**Figure 6** Predicted difference between migrant and nonmigrant rates of government employment

**Note:** The solid line is the predicted difference between migrant and nonmigrant rates of government employment, calculated using the coefficients in Table 7, Model 4. Dashed lines are for the 95 percent confidence intervals.

or diaspora funding may prop up insurgencies, for example (Salehyan 2011; Stedman and Tanner 2003; Seymour 2010).[36]

In contrast to the image of insurgents in exile, domestic migrants rarely take up arms against the state. Two scenarios are more common. Governments back migration to the periphery, and the state tolerates or abets violence by settlers against locals. Alternately, migrants are targeted by nativists who resent the incursion and competition for resources. According to Fearon and Laitin (2011), violence against migrants can be an opening salvo in a civil war between the government and sons-of-the-soil. In this kind of war, the rebels are drawn from a regionally based ethnic group with grievances related to migration to their area. The state is, at least initially, aligned with the migrants. Relatively unorganized violence by nativists, such as riots and pogroms, draws the state into guerrilla war when it deploys security forces to protect migrants in the periphery.

---

[36] Although instances of refugee or diaspora cooperation with insurgencies are well documented, Shaver and Zhou (2017) suggest that the average effect of refugee flows is to reduce conflict.

In this section, we show that internal migration spurs rioting in migrant destinations. We do so in two steps, first showing that subnational migration and riots are indeed positively correlated across all the developing and transitional countries and regions on which we can obtain migration and violence data (these are 526 regions in twenty-one countries across Asia and Africa). To confirm the causal effect of migration on unrest, we turn to a natural experiment in India, showing that natural disaster-induced migration in the country causes riots. Consistent with our theory and finding that decentralization in India allows states to favor natives, presented in Section 3, India's recent political decentralization attenuated the effects of migration on rioting.

## 4.1 Migration and Rioting Across Hundreds of Regions in Twenty-one Countries

We have argued that growing internal migration is frequently met by anti-migrant violence. To test this hypothesis, we combine data on internal migration from the IMAGE database with data on rioting from the Armed Conflict Location and Event Data (ACLED) project. The resulting data set is a cross section of more than 500 subnational units across twenty-one countries: five in Asia (Cambodia, India, Malaysia, Thailand, and Vietnam), three in North Africa (Egypt, Morocco, and Tunisia), and thirteen in Sub-Saharan Africa (Burkina Faso, Cameroon, Ghana, Guinea, Kenya, Malawi, Mali, Rwanda, Senegal, Sudan, Tanzania, Uganda, and Zambia).[37]

The ACLED database reports violent events across Africa and Asia and includes information on the type of violence (battles, riots, etc.) and its location. For our analysis, we use data on riots and aggregate these to the subnational units for which we have migration data. For ACLED, a "protest describes a non-violent, group public demonstration, often against a government institution. Rioting is a violent form of demonstration" (ACLED 2017: 9). A note on timing: the migration data in the IMAGE database are cross sectional. Where possible, these migration data were matched with contemporaneous riot data from the ACLED database. When riot data were missing, migration data were matched with data on riots from later years. The resulting dependent variable is log annual average riots in an administrative unit.[38]

To gauge the effect of migration on nativist violence, we measured rioting broadly defined, rather than trying to identify anti-migrant riots in particular.

---

[37] The latest version of the ACLED database covers sixty countries, and the IMAGE database covers fifty-six countries. Twenty-one developing countries appear in both data sets.

[38] In regressions, we weight each observation by the number of years of ACLED data that were averaged to produce the dependent variable, similar to the procedure in Bhavnani and Lacina (2015).

Rioters can have multiple motivations. Data sets on war "generally rely on the official statements of belligerents to code the issues at stake. The same procedure is not possible when observing riots, since participants rarely issue statements about their reasons for rioting" (Bhavnani and Lacina 2015: p. 771). Descriptions of rioters' motives in primary and secondary sources are inherently political (Wilkinson 2004; Brass 1997). In other words, whether a riot is coded as being anti-migrant, anti-Christian, anti-Oromo, and so forth is influenced by or endogenous to the political process. For example, in 1986, there were riots in New Delhi involving Punjabi Sikhs, who were both religious minorities and migrants. The *Times of India* reported on October 27 that the riots began when "a group of Punjab migrants took to the streets" (TOI News Service 1986b), whereas the next day's report in the same paper referred to "communal" riots (TOI News Service 1986a). The available data also do not specify the responsibility for initiating violence, nor do they allow us to pinpoint the role of the government in the riots. The possible state roles run the gamut. Riots can be thinly veiled state actions, can unfold without interference from a passive or incapable government, or rioters can be met with state repression. Our limited ability to characterize the nature of riots in the ACLED data should be kept in mind throughout the analysis.

Figure 7 shows the relationship between subnational migration and riots across all 526 regions and twenty-one countries in our data. Both the scatter and fitted line describe a clearly positive relationship between riots and migration. The fitted line is equivalent to the results of a bivariate regression of migration and riots. The slope implies that a 10 percent increase in migration is associated with a 3.3 percent increase in riots.

Figure 8 disaggregates this relationship by country. The pattern is strikingly consistent across continents and countries. In eighteen of twenty-one countries, the bivariate relationship between riots and migration is positive. The exceptions are Malaysia and Guinea, where ACLED does not record any riots in the relevant years, and Senegal, where the relationship between riots and migration is weakly negative.

The association between subnational migration and riots within country regions is robust to multivariate analysis (Table 8). Model 1 examines the correlation between internal migration and riots while controlling for country fixed effects. These fixed effects control for country features such as regime type and state strength. This specification suggests that 10 percent more internal migration is correlated with 2.7 percent more rioting. In Model 2, we perform a robustness check. As noted earlier, riot

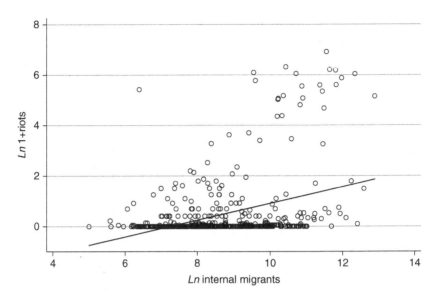

**Figure 7** Scatterplot of riots and internal migration in subnational regions of Africa, South Asia, and Southeast Asia, with the line of best fit

**Note:** Data are for countries in Asia (Cambodia, India, Malaysia, Thailand, and Vietnam), North Africa (Egypt, Morocco, and Tunisia), and Sub-Saharan Africa (Burkina Faso, Cameroon, Ghana, Guinea, Kenya, Malawi, Mali, Rwanda, Senegal, Sudan, Tanzania, Uganda, and Zambia). Riot data are from the ACLED database; migration data are from the IMAGE database. See text for details.

data are not available for some countries for the same period as our migration data. Instead, we observe riots in one or two subsequent years depending on available data. Model 2 confines the analysis to only the countries for which we have contemporaneous migration and ACLED data. Migration is statistically significant, with 10 percent more migration predicting a 0.5 percent increase in annual rioting.

Models 3 and 4 control for PPP-adjusted GDP per capita, logged population, and logged population density in each subnational unit. Controlling for GDP per capita is important because it might affect both migration (because migrants are attracted to richer regions) and riots (opportunity costs and the strength of the state are higher in richer regions). Controlling for population and population density is important because they measure resource competition, which could affect both riots and migration. Model 3 includes all countries, and Model 4 includes those for which we have contemporaneous

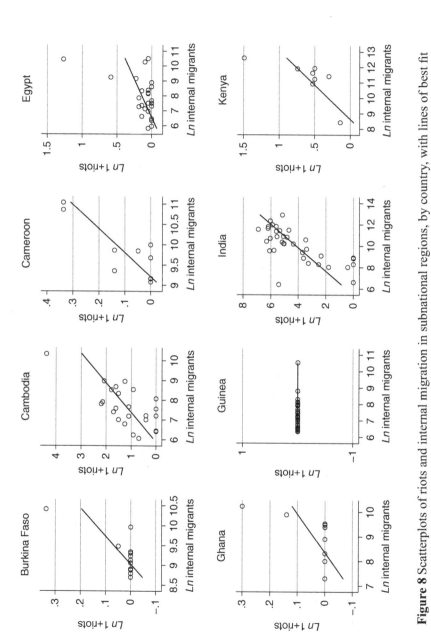

**Figure 8** Scatterplots of riots and internal migration in subnational regions, by country, with lines of best fit

**Note:** Riot data are from the ACLED database; migration data are from the IMAGE database. See text for details.

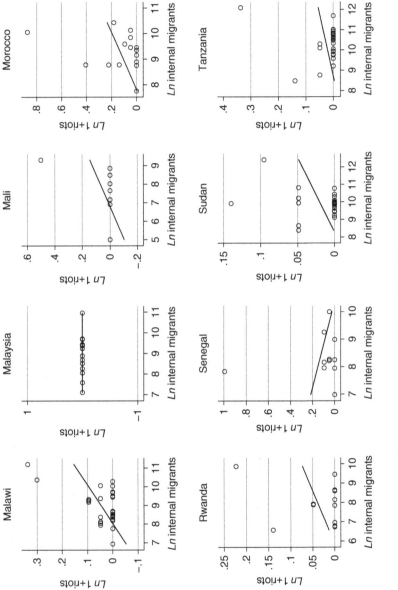

**Figure 8** (cont.)

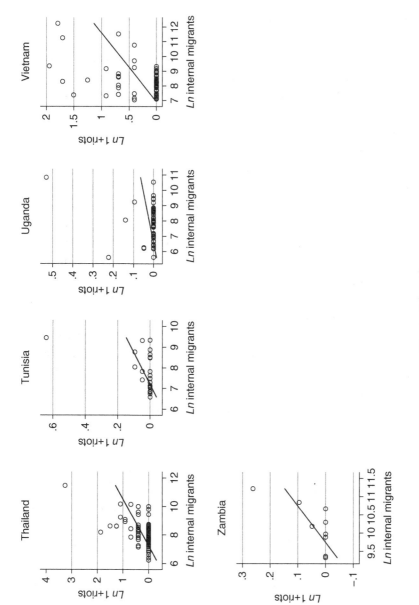

**Figure 8** (cont.)

migration and riot data. The positive relationship between migration and rioting is apparent, although slightly attenuated, in each model.

The final models in Table 8 interact migration and decentralization using a measure of subnational elections coded by Cruz, Keefer, and Scartascini (2016).[39] Decentralization is an endogenous variable. The analysis here is not causal but only captures the heterogeneous correlation between migration and riots as decentralization varies. In Model 5, the positive correlation between migration and rioting is apparent for both centralized and decentralized countries, more so in the latter, but is not statistically significant. Nor is the difference between the two coefficients for migration in Model 5 statistically significant. Also, Model 6, which uses only our highest-quality data, points in the other direction. There is a positive relationship between migration and rioting regardless of whether a country is decentralized. In countries without decentralization, however, the correlation is more than three times larger.[40] We have suggested that decentralization promotes sons-of-the-soil politics but that, by empowering nativists, it may also prevent anti-migrant violence by rendering it redundant. The mixed results of Models 5 and 6 are consistent with this ambiguity.

Bivariate and multivariate analyses of subnational data on migration and riots across twenty-one countries suggest that within-country migration might prompt nativist violence. Migration is endogenous to violence insofar as migrants choose less violent destinations, and omitted factors cause both migration and violence. Decentralization is also not an exogenous force. In some countries, such as Kenya, decentralized institutions were adopted in the midst of struggles over sons-of-the-soil politics with an eye to relieving these grievances. To more clearly expose the impact of migration, with and without decentralization, we return to the case of India.

## 4.2 Causal Evidence from a Natural Experiment in India

Subnational data from India further confirm the relationship between migration and rioting. We measure migration at the state level and show that domestic population inflows cause rioting (this subsection draws on Bhavnani and Lacina 2015). Like the analysis of the Shiv Sena in Section 3, we use disaster-induced migration as a source of exogenous variation in population movements. If migrants select into places with less violence, failing to account for the endogeneity of migrants would cause us to underestimate their effects in prompting riots.

---

[39] See also Beck et al. (2001). For missing countries, we used data from Bohlken (2016), The Hunger Project (2014), and US Department of the Army (2003).

[40] Again, however, the difference between the coefficients on migration without decentralization and migration with decentralization are not statistically significant.

**Table 8** Multivariate OLS Analysis of the Association between Riots and Internal Migration Across Subnational Regions of Twenty-one Countries

| | Model 1 | Model 2 | Model 3 | Model 4 | Model 5 | Model 6 |
|---|---|---|---|---|---|---|
| Ln internal migrants | 0.27** | 0.054*** | 0.092** | 0.034** | | |
| | (0.12) | (0.017) | (0.035) | (0.016) | | |
| Ln migrants × no political decentralization | | | | | 0.022 | 0.047** |
| | | | | | (0.060) | (0.018) |
| Ln migrants × political decentralization | | | | | 0.15 | 0.017 |
| | | | | | (0.086) | (0.012) |
| Only contemporaneous | N | Y | N | Y | N | Y |
| Country dummies | Y | Y | Y | Y | Y | Y |
| Controls | N | N | Y | Y | Y | Y |
| Observations | 526 | 280 | 526 | 280 | 526 | 280 |
| Adjusted $R^2$ | 0.76 | 0.35 | 0.79 | 0.28 | 0.79 | 0.29 |

**Note:** Control variables are PPP-adjusted GDP per capita, logged population, and logged population density. Standard errors, clustered by country, in parentheses. $*p < 0.1$; $**p < 0.05$; $***p < 0.01$.

Our analysis includes twenty-five Indian states and the National Capital Territory of Delhi, which has had a locally elected legislature and chief minister since 1994.[41] Consistent with the analysis in Section 3, we instrument for each Indian state's in-migration with population- and distance-weighted abnormal rainfall in other Indian states. (In Section 3, we instrumented migration into each of Maharashtra's districts with abnormal rainfall in other states). We measure rainfall outside the area where we want to predict conflict and use these shocks to the supply of migrants to instrument for population inflows. This strategy avoids a major problem faced by studies that use disasters to instrument for economic conditions in the area of the disaster, namely the many pathways – including migration – by which natural disasters may influence conflict (Sarsons 2015). Our empirical strategy sidesteps this problem because our instrument is not disasters in the area of study but rather disasters in migrant-sending areas.

Figure 9 is a scatterplot of the instrument and migration data (both have been "partialled out" using the controls described later), with a line of best fit. As expected, the monsoon instrument is positively correlated ($\rho = 0.3$) with average annual in-migration. In India, excess and deficient rainfall in parts of the country pushes migrants into other areas.

Our dependent variable is riot data collected by the government of India (National Crime Records Bureau 2001). Rioting is defined to encompass any group of five or more people that "uses force or violence in pursuit of a common aim."[42] Rioting is transformed into the average number of riots per year in a state period. While the theories that we are testing concern violence by natives against outsiders, our dependent variable measures all rioting. Our experience coding political violence in India convinced us that media sources were both politicized and erratic in their discussion of the sons-of-the-soil aspects of riots.

We turn the riot data into an annual average to correspond with the Indian Census data on migration. As noted in Section 3, the census categorizes residency by time intervals, implicitly defining a series of unequal periods and in-migration in each of them. Both migration and rioting are calculated as annual averages calculated over periods of unequal length.[43]

---

[41] Union territories without self-rule are excluded from our analysis. References to states should be taken to include Delhi.

[42] See Wilkinson (2004, appendix A) for a description of how government riot data are collected and their limitations.

[43] Throughout our statistical analysis, we use analytic weighting to account for the fact that some observations are the means of longer periods of time than others.

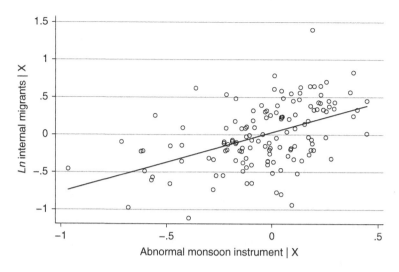

**Figure 9** Scatterplot of internal migration into India's states and abnormal
monsoon instrument, 1982–2000, with the line of best fit

**Note:** Control variables, measured for the host state, are abnormal monsoon rainfall,
land degradation, income per capita, trade flows from other states, population, urbanization among the native population, native male children's school enrollment rates, the
share of the native male population aged fifteen to nineteen years, and state fixed effects.

### 4.2.1 The Effect of Migration on Riots in India

We start our analysis of the effect of subnational migration in India by examining
the bivariate relationship between migration and riots (Model 1, Table 9; full
results are provided in Appendix Table S6). The two variables are positively
correlated, the same pattern seen in the subnational data from twenty-one countries
earlier.

In Model 2, we control for an overlapping but richer set of controls than we
were able to use in the twenty-one-country analysis. We control for income per
capita, population, urbanization, native male children's school enrollment
rates, and the share of the native male population aged fifteen to nineteen
years. These variables are associated with economic competition, which
might affect both migration and violence. We additionally control for possible
links between our abnormal monsoon rainfall instrument and violence that do
not run through migration. Two of these variables were also used in Section 3:
abnormal monsoons in the place where we observe our dependent variable and
land degradation. At the state-year level we can also control for economic

spillovers that might be caused by abnormal monsoons: trade flows from other Indian states. Lastly, our analysis uses state fixed effects, thereby controlling for time-invariant factors such as culture that might help explain our independent and dependent variables. On controlling for this rich set of possible confounds, we find that the estimated effect of migration on riots remains positive and statistically significant.

Lastly, we switch to 2SLS, to confirm that the positive relationship between internal migration and riots is indeed causal (Model 3). The first-stage regression suggests that abnormal monsoon rainfall does indeed cause migration into India's states. The first-stage $F$-statistic is 32, well above the informal threshold of 10 for strong instrumentation. The estimated effect of migration on riots is positive and statistically significant, with a 10 percent increase in migration causing a 5.6 percent increase in riots. In India, internal migration causes riots.

In this subsection we have shown that exogenous shocks to migration are met with politicized violence in India. As we have described previously, this violence is a part of a broader nativist backlash against migration. Although we do not formally test whether this backlash indeed "works" to reduce migration, we note that riots in Indian states are negatively correlated with subsequent in-migration.[44] Another piece of evidence that riots attenuate migration can be seen by comparing Models 2 and 3 of Table 9. In the latter, which accounts for the endogeneity of migration and riots, the estimated effect of migration on riots is almost doubled. We would expect this kind of downward bias in the naive correlation between migration and riots if violence or the risk of violence deters migrants.

## 4.3 The Attenuating Effect of India's Decentralization

Political decentralization has an ambiguous effect on the relationship between migration and nativist violence. On the one hand, political decentralization creates and empowers subnational governments and politicians with incentives to define and cater to locals over others. Political decentralization might therefore facilitate anti-migrant violence. On the other hand, decentralization might attenuate nativist violence by empowering local politicians to discriminate against migrants. This structural violence renders physical violence redundant. In Section 3, we found that the decentralization reforms that were implemented in India after 1993 decreased the chances that migrants are government employees. In other words, decentralization creates governments that cater to natives rather than migrants. If decentralization leads to pro-native policies, it might lessen the "need" for costly violence. In other words, political

---

[44] Controlling for the standard control set described earlier, including state fixed effects.

**Table 9** Multivariate OLS and 2SLS Analysis of the Effects of Internal Migration on Riots in India

| | OLS Model 1 | OLS Model 2 | 2SLS Model 3 | | OLS Model 4 |
| | | | First stage | Second stage | |
| --- | --- | --- | --- | --- | --- |
| *Ln* internal migrants | 0.92*** | 0.31* | | 0.56*** | |
| | (0.20) | (0.16) | | (0.22) | |
| Abnormal monsoon instrument | | | 0.84*** | | |
| | | | (0.15) | | |
| *Ln* internal migrants × no political decentralization | | | | | 0.30** |
| | | | | | (0.14) |
| *Ln* internal migrants × political decentralization | | | | | 0.19 |
| | | | | | (0.11) |
| Political decentralization | | | | | 1.5 |
| | | | | | (1.3) |
| State dummies | N | Y | Y | Y | Y |

**Table 9** (cont.)

| | OLS Model 1 | OLS Model 2 | 2SLS Model 3 First stage | 2SLS Model 3 Second stage | OLS Model 4 |
|---|---|---|---|---|---|
| Controls | N | Y | Y | Y | Y |
| Observations | 138 | 138 | 138 | 138 | 138 |
| Adjusted $R^2$ | 0.38 | 0.95 | | | 0.95 |
| First-stage $F$-statistic | | | 32 | | |
| Second-stage $F$-statistic | | | | 720 | |

**Note:** Control variables, measured for the host state, are abnormal monsoon rainfall, land degradation, income per capita, trade flows from other states, population, urbanization among the native population, native male children's school enrollment rates, and the share of the native male population aged fifteen to nineteen years. Standard errors, clustered by state, in parentheses. $*p < 0.1$; $**p < 0.05$; $***p < 0.01$.

decentralization might substitute state discrimination and official coercion against migrants for nonstate nativist violence.

To test the possibility that decentralization does indeed lessen the degree of rioting that migration prompts, we follow the cross-national analysis in Table 8 and interact migration with dummies for no political decentralization and political decentralization. We include these terms in our OLS specification with controls, although the statistically significant relationship between migration and violence in states without decentralization is robust to using 2SLS (see Appendix Table S7).[45] As before, we emphasize that this is an analysis of the heterogeneous effects of migration as decentralization varies rather than a causal analysis of the effects of decentralization per se. The results (Model 4 of Table 9) suggest that a 10 percent increase in migration prompts a 3 percent increase in riots in places with no political decentralization. The estimated effect of migration on riots in places with political decentralization is smaller and statistically insignificant. The difference between the coefficient on migration in decentralized and undecentralized places is not statistically significant. Overall, the data are consistent with the idea that decentralization shifts government policy in favor of natives and decreases the chances of nativists taking up violence outside of state channels.

We have leveraged the phased implementation of decentralization reforms across India's states to examine how the increased empowerment of nativist politicians affects employment discrimination against migrants and riots. In Section 3.3, we showed that decentralization prompted increased anti-migrant discrimination in government employment. In this section, we showed that migration into decentralized states simultaneously failed to prompt riots, thereby suggesting that discrimination and riots are sometimes substitutes. Future work should examine how state discrimination and coercion reinforce or replace nonstate violence.

## 4.4 Conclusions

In this section, we examined the link between internal migration and rioting. Using new, detailed subnational migration data from over 500 regions across twenty-one developing countries in Asia, North Africa, and Sub-Saharan Africa, we have shown that in-migration is associated with an increase in riots. This pattern is evident in the raw data both within and across countries

---

[45] In the 2SLS model, there is no statistically significant difference in the estimated coefficients on "*Ln* internal migrants × no political decentralization" and "*Ln* internal migrants × political decentralization." In contrast to the results in Table 9, however, the point estimate is larger on the latter variable. We deemphasize this 2SLS analysis because it is inadvisable to instrument for more than one endogenous variable (Angrist and Pischke 2009: 64–66).

and is robust to controlling for possible confounds. We leverage a natural experiment due to monsoon-induced migration in India and confirm that the relationship between migration and one form of nonstate violence is indeed causal. Exogenous, natural disaster-induced migration shocks cause riots in migrant-receiving states.

In Section 3, we showed that political decentralization facilitated the redirection of government jobs to natives over migrants. Consistent with the possibility that discrimination substitutes for anti-migrant riots, we find that India's decentralization attenuated the effects of migration on rioting.

Rioting is an extreme version of the hostility to internal migration across the developing world. Particularly under conditions of decentralization, subnational politicians can win by railing against outsiders. Politicians also direct resources away from migrants and state coercion toward them. These patterns are remarkably similar to the reaction in the Organisation for Economic Cooperation and Development (OECD) to international migrants. What, then, can countries do to handle internal migrants better? We turn to this question in our next and final section.

## 5 Integration and Nativism: Averting the Collision

Few doubt the political salience of international migration in Europe and North America. In the coming decades, however, an equal or greater challenge for global security and prosperity will be conflict over migration within the developing world. Falling transportation costs, information technologies, and economic liberalization bring subnational regions, as well as countries, into closer economic relationships. Climate change will speed the redistribution of people within countries.

Internal migration is politically fraught in developing countries. Compared with industrialized countries, developing countries have much larger geographic disparities in household incomes. These disparities coexist with weaker national identities and greater ethnic and religious diversity. Many ethnic groups span porous international borders, which blurs the distinction between domestic and foreign migration. As a practical matter, many developing states lack the administrative capacity to distinguish citizens and noncitizens. A government crackdown on foreign migrants will sweep up citizens from the targeted ethnic group. The reverse holds as well. Postcommunist and postcolonial countries share recent histories of regulating internal migration and creating sons-of-the-soil rights in some administrative areas. These institutions can be co-opted and strengthened by nativists to deter migrants and ensure preferential treatment for locals.

At the same time that migration is surging, a majority of developing countries have implemented some form of political decentralization. Subnational elections increase the chances that internal migration becomes politically relevant. Movements between arenas of political competition are more controversial than movements across merely administrative borders. Internal nativism is often a winning political strategy in localized contests.

This Element has woven together evidence on the effects of internal migration from all over the developing world. We have highlighted data on party competition and violence from India. For that country, we have powerful tools of causal identification. We use monsoon disasters to isolate exogenous shocks to internal migration. We use the staggered introduction of substate elections to study how the timing of decentralization changed government discrimination against migrants. Cross-national data from Latin America, Sub-Saharan Africa, and Asia yield patterns similar to what we see in India. Migration encourages sons-of-the-soil parties to form and bolsters their electoral fortunes. It also spurs rioting. Decentralization strengthens the connection between migration and the success of sons-of-the-soil politicking but does not necessarily aggravate nativist violence.

We have sought to make several contributions here. First, although many works have argued that internal migration prompts a backlash, most focus on places that have experienced sons-of-the-soil violence, with less regard for instances when migration has been benign. The literature as a whole therefore "selects on the dependent variable." Given this, a major contribution of this Element is its cross- and subnational focus. By examining the effects of migration across all the developing-country regions for which we could find data (for the riots outcome, this was 526 regions in twenty-one developing countries), we are able to better examine whether internal migration is indeed associated with a backlash.

A second contribution is that we are able to use two natural experiments in India to make stronger causal claims than much of the literature has been able to make thus far. We examine the causal effect of migration on an archetypal sons-of-the-soil party, the Shiv Sena, using a natural experiment due to disaster-induced migration in India. A similar design allows us to show that migration causes riots in India. In addition, we are able to use the constitutionally mandated and staggered decentralization of the Indian states to examine the degree to which decentralization facilitates or quells anti-migrant discrimination and violence.

Our third contribution is to bring the literatures on sons-of-the-soil politics into conversation with the literatures on decentralization and international migration. As we have argued and shown, decentralization facilitates a political backlash against migration. This is an unappreciated dynamic in the sons-of-the-soil literature and theories of decentralization. Lastly, we have also sought to connect the large literature on the effects of international migration in the OECD to the smaller literature on sons-of-the-soil politics in developing countries.

## 5.1 Managing Migration

Policymakers need to be cognizant of domestic nativism because it is a formidable political barrier to realizing the human and economic promises of integration. Domestic migration is widely accepted as a human right. Without migration, people lose one tool for holding the government accountable because they cannot "vote with their feet." Economic integration holds great promise for development. Internal movement is also spurred by factors beyond any one state's control, like enhanced communications technology and climate change. How can policymakers prevent a collision between integration of markets and nativism? How can scholars interested in migration, governance, and violence adapt their research to answer this question?

One research frontier is to examine why some places are more resilient to subnational nativism than others. For example, Bhavnani and Lacina (2015, 2017) argue that political parties are a key institution that mediates the relationship between migration and nativism. When compared with rich countries, the developing world has a much wider range of political and economic systems. Much more work is needed to characterize formal and informal institutions that prevent sons-of-the-soil conflict.

Where domestic nativism is likely, what interventions will prevent violence and maintain political support for openness among locals? Some of the policies that address sons-of-the-soil demands are pernicious. State repression may keep nativist activists in check or block migration. Protectionist and nativist policies (de jure or de facto) roll back labor market integration. More benign policies might compensate people for the stresses caused by internal migration. Central governments can redistribute resources to host areas to expand infrastructure and cope with migration (Bhavnani and Lacina 2017). There is also a clear case for reducing disparities in public services across regions and mitigating natural disasters to prevent migration. Population movements prompted by these push factors are arguably not enhancing the efficiency of the labor market.

Should domestic nativism prompt countries to slow or reverse political decentralization? The effects of decentralization on many outcomes – growth, corruption, democratic legitimacy – are still debated (Treisman 2007). In the politics of domestic migration, decentralization has a paradoxical role, fueling nativism as it creates new arenas for political competition, empowering politicians to cater to natives, and possibly preventing nonstate nativist riots by aligning the power of the state with locals.

Thinking about decentralization in light of migration politics yields new insights for the vast literatures on fiscal federalism, market-preserving decentralization, and interjurisdictional competition. When domestic nativism is a salient political force, interactions between jurisdictions are not analogous to market competition that decreases corruption or preserves market-friendly policy. Instead, the governments of subnational jurisdictions rally constituents against out-groups and practice beggar-thy-neighbor protectionism. Domestic nativism has the potential to not only impede the integration of labor markets but also obstruct the free trade of goods and services within countries (Bhavnani and Lacina 2016).[46] Domestic trade within developing countries is frequently stifled by internal barriers such as entry or octroi taxes levied on goods or subnational variation in licensing requirements that operate as a tax on services. Such protectionist measures are an impediment to internal trade in goods in India, China, Nigeria, and even Canada and were routine in the developed West historically.

The normative justification for decentralization is based on local accountability. Critics point out that decentralized authorities may be more vulnerable to capture by special interests, may free-ride on each other in arenas such as tax efforts, and may fail to internalize externalities such as environmental pollution. Migration is a policy arena where free-riding and externalities may become a problem. In this policy arena, local, nativist, and ethnic special interests are often well placed to capture the subnational government, raising normative problems.

How can political decentralization be adapted to a context of economic integration and higher labor mobility where regional identities are politically salient? Central governments should transfer funds from place to place to ameliorate the stresses of migration and market competition. The aim should not be to equalize the spatial distribution of economic production, which would undo the benefits of agglomeration. Central governments should try to equalize incomes and services across space and between locals and migrants to mitigate the backlash against economic integration. The benefit of such interventions is well known. There is a need for research on when central governments have the political incentive to use fiscal tools to decrease nativism. For example, Riker (1964) argues that political parties that compete nationally and subnationally

---

[46] For links between migration and international trade policies, see Peters (2015).

help coordinate multilevel government action. Migration is the kind of challenge with which party ties may help politically decentralized countries deal. Our past research suggests that parties play this role in India (Bhavnani and Lacina 2015, 2017). More general investigation of Riker's thesis is newly policy relevant.

## 5.2 The Global Challenge of Nativism

Domestic nativism in developing countries throws new light on the study of migration in rich areas. We show that sons-of-the-soil politics appears in countries undergoing rapid economic growth and industrialization. Neither deindustrialization nor the retraction of a once-robust welfare state is a necessary condition for nativism. In fact, we find sons-of-the-soil politics where the economy is booming. Even people who do not compete with migrants for income may resent the changes they represent, such as urban sprawl and failing public services.

Economic flux and competition are enough to make nativism appealing. Assistance to people who perceive themselves to be losing out from economic change may be effective in fighting nativism and maintaining political support for economic integration. But general improvement in the macroeconomy is unlikely to end nativism, internal or external.

# Appendix
## *Supplementary Tables*

**Table S1** Countries in the IMAGE Data Set with Less
Developed and Transitional Economies

| Country | Migration data |
|---|---|
| Argentina | 2001 |
| Barbados | 2000 |
| Bolivia | 2001 |
| Brazil | 2000 |
| Burkina Faso | 2006 |
| Cambodia | 1998 |
| Cameroon | 2005 |
| Chile | 2002 |
| China | 2000 |
| Colombia | 2005 |
| Costa Rica | 2000 |
| Cuba | 2002 |
| Dominican Republic | 2010 |
| Ecuador | 2001 |
| Egypt | 2006 |
| El Salvador | 2007 |
| Estonia | 2010 |
| Fiji | 2007 |
| Ghana | 2000 |
| Guatemala | 2002 |
| Guinea | 1996 |
| Haiti | 2003 |
| Honduras | 2001 |
| India | 2001 |
| Indonesia | 2010 |
| Iran | 2011 |

**Table S1** (cont.)

| Country | Migration data |
|---|---|
| Iraq | 1997 |
| Kenya | 1999 |
| Kyrgyzstan | 1999 |
| Malawi | 2008 |
| Malaysia | 2000 |
| Mali | 1998 |
| Mauritius | 2000 |
| Mexico | 2010 |
| Mongolia | 2000 |
| Morocco | 2004 |
| Nicaragua | 2005 |
| North Korea | 2008 |
| Panama | 2000 |
| Paraguay | 2002 |
| Peru | 2007 |
| Poland | 2010 |
| Rwanda | 2002 |
| Senegal | 2002 |
| Sudan | 2008 |
| Tanzania | 2002 |
| Thailand | 2000 |
| Tunisia | 2004 |
| Turkey | 2012 |
| Uganda | 2002 |
| Ukraine | 2010 |
| Uruguay | 2011 |
| Venezuela | 2011 |
| Vietnam | 2009 |
| Zambia | 2000 |

**Table S2** Full Results of Models in Table 4

| | Ln % seats with Sena candidate | | | | Ln % Sena vote | Ln % Sena seats |
| | OLS | OLS | 2SLS Model 3 | | 2SLS Model 4 | 2SLS Model 5 |
| | Model 1 | Model 2 | First stage | Second stage | Second stage | Second stage |
|---|---|---|---|---|---|---|
| Ln out-of-state migrants | 0.37*** | 0.67** | | 5.9*** | 3.959*** | 1.7** |
| | (0.10) | (0.24) | | (0.91) | (0.67)*** | (0.79) |
| Abnormal monsoon instrument | | | 1.6*** | | | |
| | | | (0.27) | | | |
| Abnormal monsoon rainfall | | 0.056 | 0.071 | −1.3* | −0.94** | −0.27 |
| | | (0.44) | (0.12) | (0.66) | (0.44) | (0.46) |
| Ln % degraded land | | 0.37 | −0.20* | 1.5** | 0.88** | 0.48 |
| | | (0.30) | (0.11) | (0.61) | (0.39) | (0.33) |
| Ln income per capita | | −3.2* | 0.71 | −8.3*** | −5.1*** | −2.4** |
| | | (1.7) | (0.44) | (2.1) | (1.3) | (1.1) |
| Ln native state population | | 10** | −0.0805 | 9.221 | 5.410 | 4.445 |
| | | (4.6) | (1.3) | (8.5) | (5.5) | (3.6) |

Table S2 (cont.)

| | Ln % seats with Sena candidate | | | | Ln % Sena vote | Ln % Sena seats |
| | OLS | OLS | 2SLS Model 3 | | 2SLS Model 4 | 2SLS Model 5 |
| | Model 1 | Model 2 | First stage | Second stage | Second stage | Second stage |
|---|---|---|---|---|---|---|
| Ln % urbanization | | 2.414 | 1.5** | −6.4 | −3.8 | 1.4 |
| | | (2.1) | (0.69) | (4.2) | (2.8) | (2.2) |
| Ln % male children's school enrollment | | 4.0 | −0.231 | 0.46 | −0.48 | −0.56 |
| | | (3.4) | (1.5) | (8.7) | (5.9) | (3.0) |
| Ln % aged 15–24 years | | −3.4 | −1.7 | 5.9 | 5.4 | 6.4 |
| | | (4.1) | (1.7) | (10) | (7.1) | (4.7) |
| District dummies | N | Y | Y | Y | Y | Y |
| Observations | 129 | 129 | 129 | 129 | 129 | 129 |
| Adjusted $R^2$ | 0.08 | 0.35 | | | | |
| First-stage $F$-statistic | | | 34 | | | |
| Second-stage $F$-statistic | | | | 14 | 9 | 1 |

**Note:** Standard errors, clustered by district, in parentheses. $*p < 0.1$; $**p < 0.05$; $***p < 0.01$.

**Table S3** Full Results of Models in Table 6

|  | **Model 1** | **Model 2** | **Model 3** |
|---|---|---|---|
| *Ln* migrants | 0.13** | 0.12** | |
| | (0.0385) | (0.0426) | |
| *Ln* migrants × political decentralization | | | 0.14* |
| | | | (0.068) |
| *Ln* migrants × no political decentralization | | | −0.11 |
| | | | (0.17) |
| Indigenous population (%) | 0.012* | 0.013** | 0.014** |
| | (0.0051) | (0.0045) | (0.0046) |
| *Ln* population density | −0.035 | −0.062 | −0.079 |
| | (0.065) | (0.076) | (0.071) |
| *Ln* GDP per capita | −0.081 | −0.088 | −0.082 |
| | (0.050) | (0.060) | (0.062) |
| *Ln* population | −0.015 | 0.018 | 0.062 |
| | (0.12) | (0.13) | (0.100) |
| Poverty (%) | | −0.0076 | −0.0098 |
| | | (0.0077) | (0.0064) |
| *Ln* left party vote share$_{t=0}$ | | 0.0037 | 0.0036 |
| | | (0.11) | (0.11) |
| District magnitude$_{t=1}$ | | −0.0014* | −0.0019** |
| | | (0.00059) | (0.00052) |
| Country dummies | Y | Y | Y |
| Observations | 124 | 124 | 124 |
| Adjusted $R^2$ | 0.87 | 0.87 | 0.87 |

**Note:** Standard errors, clustered by country, in parentheses. *$p < 0.1$; **$p < 0.05$; ***$p < 0.01$.

**Table S4** Full Results of Models in Table 7

|  | **Model 1** | **Model 2** | **Model 3** | **Model 4** |
|---|---|---|---|---|
| Migrant × political decentralization | −0.016** (0.0073) | −0.015** (0.0061) | | |
| Migrant × years decentralized | | | −0.0030** (0.0013) | −0.0028** (0.0012) |
| Out-of-state migrant | 0.0074 (0.0054) | 0.0068 (0.0048) | 0.0069 (0.0052) | 0.0064 (0.0047) |
| Political decentralization | −0.0011 (0.0020) | | | |
| Years decentralized | | | 0.00011 (0.000360) | |
| Urban | 0.022*** (0.0023) | 0.022*** (0.0014) | 0.022*** (0.0023) | 0.022*** (0.0014) |
| Male | 0.029*** (0.0023) | 0.029*** (0.0014) | 0.029*** (0.0023) | 0.029*** (0.0014) |
| Age | 0.00079*** (0.000059) | 0.00079*** (0.000042) | 0.00079*** (0.000059) | 0.00079*** (0.000042) |
| Completed primary school | 0.016*** (0.0016) | 0.016*** (0.0013) | 0.016*** (0.0017) | 0.016*** (0.0013) |
| Completed secondary school | 0.058*** (0.0045) | 0.058*** (0.0040) | 0.058*** (0.0045) | 0.058*** (0.0040) |
| Postsecondary degree | 0.0949*** (0.0086) | 0.0948*** (0.0065) | 0.0949*** (0.0086) | 0.0948*** (0.0065) |
| State dummies | Y | N | Y | N |
| Year dummies | Y | N | Y | N |
| State-year dummies | N | Y | N | Y |
| Observations | 965,325 | 965,325 | 965,325 | 965.325 |
| Adjusted $R^2$ | 0.06 | 0.06 | 0.06 | 0.06 |

**Note:** Standard errors, clustered by state (Models 1 and 2) or state-year (Models 3 and 4), in parentheses. $*p < 0.1$; $**p < 0.05$; $***p < 0.01$.

**Table S5** Full Results of Models in Table 8

| | Model 1 | Model 2 | Model 3 | Model 4 | Model 5 | Model 6 |
|---|---|---|---|---|---|---|
| Ln internal migrants | 0.27** | 0.054*** | 0.092** | 0.034** | | |
| | (0.12) | (0.017) | (0.035) | (0.016) | | |
| Ln migrants × no political decentralization | | | | | 0.022 | 0.047** |
| | | | | | (0.060) | (0.018) |
| Ln migrants × political decentralization | | | | | 0.15 | 0.017 |
| | | | | | (0.086) | (0.012) |
| Ln GDP per capita | | | 0.0037 | 0.0010 | 0.0041 | -0.00013 |
| | | | (0.0080) | (0.0048) | (0.0087) | (0.0058) |
| Ln population | | | 0.28 | -0.010 | 0.28 | -0.012 |
| | | | (0.18) | (0.015) | (0.16) | (0.016) |
| Ln population density | | | -0.058 | 0.036*** | -0.047 | 0.035*** |
| | | | (0.053) | (0.011) | (0.043) | (0.011) |
| Only contemporaneous | N | Y | N | Y | N | Y |
| Country dummies | Y | Y | Y | Y | Y | Y |
| Observations | 530 | 280 | 530 | 280 | 530 | 280 |
| Adjusted $R^2$ | 0.76 | 0.35 | 0.79 | 0.28 | 0.79 | 0.29 |

**Note:** Standard errors, clustered by country, in parentheses. *$p < 0.1$; **$p < 0.05$; ***$p < 0.01$.

## Table S6 Full Results of Models in Table 9

|  | OLS Model 1 | OLS Model 2 | 2SLS Model 3 First stage | 2SLS Model 3 Second stage | OLS Model 4 |
|---|---|---|---|---|---|
| *Ln* internal | 0.92*** | 0.31* |  | 0.56*** |  |
| migrants | (0.20) | (0.16) |  | (0.22) |  |
| Abnormal |  |  | 0.84*** |  |  |
| monsoon |  |  | (0.15) |  |  |
| instrument |  |  |  |  |  |
| *Ln* internal |  |  |  |  | 0.30** |
| migrants × no |  |  |  |  | (0.14) |
| political |  |  |  |  |  |
| decentralization |  |  |  |  |  |
| *Ln* internal |  |  |  |  | 0.19 |
| migrants × |  |  |  |  | (0.11) |
| political |  |  |  |  |  |
| decentralization |  |  |  |  |  |
| Political |  |  |  |  | 1.5 |
| decentralization |  |  |  |  | (1.3) |
| Abnormal |  | 0.15 | 0.39** | 0.070 | 0.23 |
| monsoon rainfall |  | (0.14) | (0.18) | (0.15) | (0.14) |
| *Ln* % degraded land |  | 0.0413 | −0.511*** | 0.151 | 0.030 |
|  |  | (0.63) | (0.19) | (0.36) | (0.65) |
| *Ln* income per |  | 0.70 | 0.73*** | 0.58 | 0.47 |
| capita |  | (0.53) | (0.23) | (0.41) | (0.51) |
| *Ln* domestic |  | −0.094 | 0.080 | −0.098 | −0.13* |
| imports per | (0.072) | (0.081) | (0.062) | (0.076) |
| capita |  |  |  |  |  |
| *Ln* state population |  | −0.57 | 0.64 | −0.75 | −1.04 |
|  |  | (1.89) | (0.69) | (1.4) | (1.92) |
| *Ln* native |  | 0.58 | 0.083 | 0.61 | 0.59 |
| urbanization (%) |  | (0.87) | (0.34) | (0.53) | (0.83) |
| *Ln* native male |  | −3.2* | −1.5 | −3.1** | −3.3* |
| children's school |  | (1.7) | (0.95) | (1.5) | (1.7) |
| enrollment (%) |  |  |  |  |  |
| *Ln* % native males |  | 0.61 | 0.20 | 0.72 | 1.3 |
| aged 15–24 |  | (2.9) | (1.0) | (1.7) | (2.7) |
| State dummies | N | Y | Y | Y | Y |

**Table S6** (cont.)

| | OLS Model 1 | OLS Model 2 | 2SLS Model 3 First stage | 2SLS Model 3 Second stage | OLS Model 4 |
|---|---|---|---|---|---|
| Observations | 138 | 138 | 138 | 138 | 138 |
| Adjusted $R^2$ | 0.38 | 0.95 | | | 0.95 |
| First-stage $F$-statistic | | | 32 | | |
| Second-stage $F$-statistic | | | | 720 | |

**Note:** Observations are for state-periods. Standard errors, clustered by state, in parentheses. $*p < 0.1$; $**p < 0.05$; $***p < 0.01$.

*Appendix*

**Table S7** 2SLS Estimate of Model 4 in Appendix Table S6

| | First stage | | |
|---|---|---|---|
| | *Ln* internal migrants × no political decentralization | *Ln* internal migrants × political decentralization | Second stage |
| Abnormal monsoon instrument × no decentralization | 0.98*** (0.23) | −0.14 (0.15) | |
| Abnormal monsoon instrument × decentralization | 0.19 (0.66) | 0.73 (0.60) | |
| *Ln* internal migrants × no political decentralization | | | 0.59*** (0.22) |
| *Ln* internal migrants × political decentralization | | | 0.81 (0.58) |
| Political decentralization | −5.3 (4.0) | 5.1 (3.7) | −1.9 (5.4) |
| Abnormal monsoon rainfall | 0.12 (0.26) | 0.30* (0.18) | 0.028 (0.25) |
| *Ln* % degraded land | 1.1** (0.47) | −1.5*** (0.40) | 0.64 (0.90) |
| *Ln* income per capita | 0.69 (0.47) | −0.092 (0.47) | 0.45 (0.35) |
| *Ln* domestic imports per capita | 0.13 (0.16) | −0.057 (0.13) | −0.091 (0.12) |
| *Ln* state population | 3.0* (1.5) | −2.5 (1.5) | −0.31 (2.3) |
| *Ln* native urbanization (%) | 0.15 (0.64) | −0.055 (0.56) | 0.63 |
| *Ln* native male children's school enrollment (%) | −2.5 (1.8) | 0.83 (1.4) | −3.4** (1.5) |
| *Ln* % native males aged 15–24 | 0.10 (1.7) | 0.49 (1.4) | 1.0 (1.9) |
| Observations | 138 | 138 | 138 |
| First-stage *F*-statistic | 9.0 | 1.1 | |
| Second-stage *F*-statistic | | | 420 |

**Note:** Observations are for state periods. Standard errors, clustered by state, in parentheses. *$p < 0.1$; **$p < 0.05$; ***$p < 0.01$.

# References

Abbas, Rameez (2016). "Internal migration and citizenship in India." *Journal of Ethnic and Migration Studies* 42(1), 150–68.

Acemoglu, Daron, and James A. Robinson (2001). "Inefficient redistribution." *American Political Science Review* 95(3), 649–61.

ACLED (2017). Armed Conflict Location & Event Data Project (ACLED) User Guide, January 2017. Available at http://www.acleddata.com/wp-content/uploads/2017/01/ACLED_User-Guide_2017.pdf (accessed June 9, 2018).

Adepoju, Aderanti (1984). "Illegals and expulsion in Africa: The Nigerian experience." *International Migration Review* 18(3), 426–36.

Adida, Claire L. (2014). *Immigrant Exclusion and Insecurity in Africa: Coethnic Strangers*. New York, NY: Cambridge University Press.

Allen, Joseph Boots (2003). "Ethnicity and inequality among migrants in the Kyrgyz Republic." *Central Eurasian Studies Review* 2(1): 7–10.

Alok, V. N. (2014). Measuring Devolution to Panchayats in India: A Comparison Across States – Empirical Assessment, 2013–14, Indian Institute of Public Administration, New Delhi. Available at www.iipa.org.in/upload /Devolution_Index_Report_2013-14.pdf (accessed July 5, 2018).

Anderson, Liam (2014). "Ethnofederalism: The worst form of institutional arrangement . . . ?" *International Security* 39(1), 165–204.

Angrist, Joshua D., and Jörn-Steffen Pischke (2009). *Mostly Harmless Econometrics: An Empiricist's Companion*. Princeton, NJ: Princeton University Press.

Auerbach, Adam Michael (2016). "Clients and communities: The political economy of party network organization and development in India's urban slums." *World Politics* 68(1), 111–48.

Barnett, Jon, and W. Neil Adger (2007). "Climate change, human security and violent conflict." *Political Geography* 26(6), 639–55.

Bates, Robert H. (1981). *States and Markets in Tropical Africa: The Political Basis of Agricultural Policies*. Berkeley, CA: University of California Press.

Beck, Thorsten, George Clarke, Alberto Groff, et al. (2001). "New tools in comparative political economy: The database of political institutions." *World Bank Economic Review* 15(1), 165–176.

Bekker, Simon, and Antoinette Louw (1994). "Conflict and migration in KwaZulu-Natal." In *Here to Stay: Informal Settlements in KwaZulu-Natal*, ed. Doug Hindson and Jeff McCarthy. Dalbridge: Indicator Press, pp. 99–106.

Bell, Martin, Konstantinos Daras, Marek Kupiszewski, John Stillwell, and Yu Zhu (2015). *Internal Migration around the GlobE (IMAGE)*. Brisbane: Queensland Centre for Population Research, University of Queensland.

Bergholt, Drago, and Päivi Lujala (2012). "Climate-related natural disasters, economic growth, and armed civil conflict." *Journal of Peace Research* 49 (1), 147–62.

Bhavnani, Rikhil R. (2009). "Do electoral quotas work after they are with-drawn? Evidence from a natural experiment in India." *American Political Science Review* 103(1), 23–35.

Bhavnani, Rikhil R. (2017). "Do the effects of temporary ethnic group quotas persist? Evidence from India." *American Economic Journal: Applied Economics* 9(3), 105–23.

Bhavnani, Rikhil R., and Bethany Lacina (2015). "The effects of weather-induced migration on sons of the soil riots in India." *World Politics* 67(4), 760–94.

Bhavnani, Rikhil R., and Bethany Lacina (2016). "Political obstacles to domestic trade: Evidence from India." Presented at the 2016 Annual Meeting of the International Political Economy Society, November 11–12, Durham, NC.

Bhavnani, Rikhil R., and Bethany Lacina (2017). "Fiscal federalism at work? Central responses to internal migration in India." *World Development* 93, 236–48.

Bhavnani, Rikhil R., and Alexander Lee (2018). "Local embeddedness and bureaucratic performance: Evidence from India." *Journal of Politics* 80(1), 71–87.

Birkeland, Nina M., Edmund Jennings, and Elizabeth J. Rushing, eds. (2012). *Global Overview 2011: People Internally Displaced by Conflict and Violence*. Geneva: Internal Displacement Monitoring Centre, Norwegian Refugee Council.

Bohlken, Anjali Thomas (2016). *Democratization from Above: The Logic of Local Democracy in the Developing World*. New York, NY: Cambridge University Press.

Bohlken, Anjali Thomas, and Ernest John Sergenti (2010). "Economic growth and ethnic violence: An empirical investigation of Hindu-Muslim riots in India." *Journal of Peace Research* 47(5), 589–600.

Boone, Catherine (2017). "Sons of the soil conflict in Africa: Institutional determinants of ethnic conflict over land." *World Development* 96, 276–93.

Brass, Paul R. (1997). *Theft of an Idol: Text and Context in the Representation of Collective Violence*. Princeton, NJ: Princeton University Press.

Brückner, Markus, and Antonio Ciccone (2011). "Rain and the democratic window of opportunity." *Econometrica* 79(3), 923–47.

Brysk, Alison, and Carol Wise (1997). "Liberalization and ethnic conflict in Latin America." *Studies in Comparative International Development* 32(2), 76–104.

Canessa, Andrew (2014). "Conflict, claim and contradiction in the new 'indigenous' state of Bolivia." *Critique of Anthropology* 34(2), 153–73.

Chan, Kam Wing, and Will Buckingham (2008). "Is China abolishing the Hukou system?" *China Quarterly* 195, 582–606.

Cole, Shawn, Andrew Healy, and Eric Werker (2012). "Do voters demand responsive governments? Evidence from Indian disaster relief." *Journal of Development Economics* 97(2), 167–81.

Colloredo-Mansfeld, Rudi, Angélica Ordoñez, Homero Paltán López, et al. (2018). "Conflicts, territories, and the institutionalization of post-agrarian economies on an expanding tourist frontier in Quilotoa, Ecuador." *World Development* 101, 441–52.

Côté, Isabelle, and Matthew I. Mitchell (2016). "Elections and "sons of the soil" conflict dynamics in Africa and Asia." *Democratization* 23(4), 657–77.

Cruz, Cesi, Philip Keefer, and Carlos Scartascini (2016). *Database of Political Institutions Codebook, 2015 Update*. Washington, DC: Inter-American Development Bank.

Cultural Survival (2012). "Indigenous Guatemalan protestors march in defense of territory." *Cultural Survival*, March 24. Available at www.culturalsurvival .org/news/indigenous-guatemalan-protestors-march-defense-territory (accessed October 10, 2017).

Dancygier, Rafaela M. (2010). *Immigration and Conflict in Europe*. New York, NY: Cambridge University Press.

DESA (2013). *Cross-National Comparisons of Internal Migration: An Update on Global Patterns and Trends*. New York, NY: United Nations Department of Economic and Social Affairs, Population Division.

DESA (2015). *World Population Policies Database*. New York, NY: United Nations Department of Economic and Social Affairs, Population Division. Available at https://esa.un.org/PopPolicy/about_database.aspx (accessed October 10, 2017).

Deshingkar, Priya, and John Farrington (2009). "A framework for understanding circular migration." In *Circular Migration and Rural Livelihood*

*Strategies in Rural India*, ed. Priya Deshingkar and John Farrington. New Delhi: Oxford University Press, pp. 1–36.

EM-DAT (2011). *EM-DAT: The OFDA/CRED International Disaster Database*. Brussels: Université Catholique de Louvain.

EVS (2015). *EVS 1981–2008 Variable Report: Longitudinal Data Files*. Leibniz: European Values Study and GESIS Data Archive for the Social Sciences.

Faetanini, Marina, and Rukmini Tankha, eds. (2013). *Social Inclusion of Internal Migrants in India*. New Delhi: UNESCO New Delhi.

Faist, Thomas, and Jeanette Schade (2013). "The climate–migration nexus: A reorientation." In *Disentangling Migration and Climate Change: Methodologies, Political Discources, and Human Rights*, ed. Thomas Faist and Jeanette Schade. Dordrecht: Springer, pp. 3–27.

Fearon, James D., and David D. Laitin (2011). "Sons of the soil, migrants, and civil war." *World Development* 39(2), 199–211.

Feler, Leo, and J. Vernon Henderson (2011). "Exclusionary policies in urban development: Under-servicing migrant households in Brazilian cities." *Journal of Urban Economics* 69(3), 253–72.

Flynn, Moya, Natalya Kosmarskaya, and Guzel Sabirova (2014). "The place of memory in understanding urban change in Central Asia: The cities of Bishkek and Ferghana." *Europe-Asia Studies* 66(9), 1501–24.

Frankel, Jeffrey A., and David Romer (1999). "Does trade cause growth?." *American Economic Review* 89(3), 379–99.

Gaikwad, Nikhar, and Gareth Nellis (2017). "The majority-minority divide in attitudes toward internal migration: Evidence from Mumbai." *American Journal of Political Science* 61(2), 456–72.

Gausset, Quentin, Justin Kenrick, and Robert Gibb (2011). "Indigeneity and autochthony: A couple of false twins?." *Social Anthropology* 19(2), 135–42.

Gavaskar, Mahesh (2010). "Mumbai's shattered mirror." *Economic and Political Weekly* 45(7), 17–22.

Girardin, Luc, Philipp Hunziker, Lars-Erik Cederman, Nils-Christian Bormann, and Manuel Vogt (2015). *GROWup: Geographical Research on War, Unified Platform*. Zurich: ETH. Available at http://growup.ethz.ch/ (accessed October 10, 2017).

Graham, Benjamin A. T., Michael K. Miller, and Kaare W. Strøm (2017). "Safeguarding democracy: Powersharing and democratic survival." *American Political Science Review* 111(4), 686–704.

Hansen, Thomas B. (2001). *Wages of Violence: Naming and Identity in Post-colonial Bombay*. Princeton, NJ: Princeton University Press.

Harmel, Robert, and John D. Robertson (1985). "Formation and success of new parties: A cross-national analysis." *International Political Science Review* 6 (4), 501–23.

Hatcher, Craig, and Susan Thieme (2016). "Institutional transition: Internal migration, the propiska, and post-socialist urban change in Bishkek, Kyrgyzstan." *Urban Studies* 53(10), 2175–91.

Holland, Alisha C. (2016). "Forbearance." *American Political Science Review* 110(2), 232–46.

Homer-Dixon, Thomas F. (1999). *Environment, Scarcity, and Violence.* Princeton, NJ: Princeton University Press.

Hooker, Juliet (2005). "Indigenous inclusion/black exclusion: Race, ethnicity and multicultural citizenship in Latin America." *Journal of Latin American Studies* 37(2), 285–310.

Housen, Tambri, Sandra Hopkins, and Jaya Earnest (2013). "A systematic review on the impact of internal remittances on poverty and consumption in developing countries: Implications for policy." *Population, Space and Place* 19(5), 610–32.

Hvalkof, Søren (2000). "Outrage in rubber and oil: Extractivism, indigenous peoples, and justice in the Upper Amazon." In *People, Plants, and Justice: The Politics of Nature Conservation*, ed. Charles Zerner. New York, NY: Columbia University Press, pp. 83–116.

IndiaStat (2000). *IndiaStat: Revealing India Statistically.* New Delhi, India: Datanet India.

Irwin, Douglas A. (2002). *Free Trade under Fire.* Princeton, NJ: Princeton University Press.

Iyer, Lakshmi, Anandi Mani, Prachi Mishra, and Petia Topalova (2012). "The power of political voice: Women's political representation and crime in India." *American Economic Journal: Applied Economics* 4(4), 165–93.

Jackson, Jean E., and Kay B. Warren (2005). "Indigenous movements in Latin America, 1992–2004: Controversies, ironies, new directions." *Annual Review of Anthropology* 34, 549–73.

Jacoby, Hanan G., and Emmanuel Skoufias (1997). "Risk, financial markets, and human capital in a developing country." *Review of Economic Studies* 64 (3), 311–35.

Jayachandran, Seema (2006). "Selling labor low: Wage responses to productivity shocks in developing countries." *Journal of Political Economy* 114(3), 538–75.

Jeffrey, Robin, Ronojoy Sen, and Pratima Singh, eds. (2012). *More than Maoism: Politics and Policies of Insurgency in South Asia*. New Delhi: Manohar.

Jha, Saumitra, Vijayendra Rao, and Michael Woolcock (2007)."Governance in the gullies: Democratic responsiveness and leadership in Delhi's slums." *World Development* 35(2), 230–46.

Kapur, D., Kishore Gawande, and Shanker Satyanath (2012). "Renewable resource shocks and conflict in India's Maoist belt." *CASI Working Paper Series* 12(2), 1–54.

King, Russell, and Ronald Skeldon (2010). "'Mind the gap!' Integrating approaches to internal and international migration." *Journal of Ethnic and Migration Studies* 36(10), 1619–46.

Kochar, Anjini (1999). "Smoothing consumption by smoothing income: Hours-of-work responses to idiosyncratic agricultural shocks in rural India." *Review of Economics and Statistics* 81(1), 50–61.

Kumar, K. S. Kavi (2011). "Climate sensitivity of Indian agriculture: Do spatial effects matter?." *Cambridge Journal of Regions, Economy & Society* 4(2), 221–35.

Kundu, Amitabh (2009). "Urbanisation and migration: An analysis of trends, patterns and policies in Asia." Human Development Report Office (HDRO), United Nations Development Programme (UNDP), Human Development Research Papers.

Lacina, Bethany (2014). "How governments shape the risk of civil violence: India's federal reorganization, 1950–56." *American Journal of Political Science* 58(3), 720–38.

Lacina, Bethany (2017). *Rival Claims: Ethnic Violence and Territorial Autonomy under Indian Federalism*. Ann Arbor, MI: University of Michigan Press.

Lama, Mahendra P. (2000). "Internal displacement in India: Causes, protection and dilemmas." *Forced Migration Review* 8, 24–26.

Lokniti (2009). *National Election Study*. New Delhi: Center for the Study of Developing Societies.

Lucas, Robert E. B. (2015). "Internal migration in developing economies: An overview." KNOMAD Working Paper 6.

Madrid, Raúl L. (2005). "Indigenous parties and democracy in Latin America." *Latin American Politics and Society* 47(4), 161–79.

Mall, R. K., A. Gupta, L. S. Rathore, R. Singh, and R. S. Singh (2006). "Water resources and climate change: An Indian perspective." *Current Science* 90 (12), 1610–26.

Margalit, Yotam (2011). "Costly jobs: Trade-related layoffs, government compensation, and voting in U.S. elections." *American Political Science Review* 105(1), 166–88.

McKenna, Thomas M. (1998). *Muslim Rulers and Rebels: Everyday Politics and Armed Separatism in the Southern Philippines*. Berkeley, CA: University of California Press.

McPhaul, John (2015). "Costa Rica struggles with indigenous land rights." *The Tico Times*. October 7.

McSweeney, Kendra, and Brad Jokisch (2007). "Beyond rainforests: Urbanisation and emigration among lowland indigenous societies in Latin America." *Bulletin of Latin American Research* 26(2), 159–80.

Mehlum, Halvor, Edward Miguel, and Ragnar Torvik (2006). "Poverty and crime in 19th century Germany." *Journal of Urban Economics* 59(3), 370–88.

Mendelsohn, Robert, Ariel Dinar, and Apurva Sanghi (2001). "The effect of development on the climate sensitivity of agriculture." *Environment and Development Economics* 6(1), 85–101.

Mendola, Mariapia (2012). "Rural out-migration and economic development at origin: A review of the evidence." *Journal of International Development* 24 (1), 102–22.

Miguel, Edward, Shanker Satyanath, and Ernest Sergenti (2004). "Economic shocks and civil conflict: An instrumental variables approach." *Journal of Political Economy* 112(4), 725–53.

Millward, James A. (2009). "Introduction: Does the 2009 Urumchi violence mark a turning point?." *Central Asian Ethnicity* 28(4), 347–60.

Montgomery, Mark R. (2008). "The urban transformation of the developing world." *Science* 319(5864), 761–64.

MOSPI (2012). *Manual on Labour Statistics I – 2012*. New Delhi: Government of India, Ministry of Statistics and Programme Implementation, Central Statistics Office.

National Crime Records Bureau (2001). *Crime in India, 2001*. New Delhi: Ministry of Home Affairs (India) and Government of India Press.

NCIC (2016). *Ethnic and Diversity Audit of the County Public Service*. Nairobi: National Cohesion and Integration Commission.

NSS (2010). "Migration in India, 2007–2008." NSS report no. 533, National Sample Survey Office, Ministry of Statistics and Programme Implementation, New Delhi.

Palshikar, Suhas (2010). "In the midst of sub-democratic politics." *Economic and Political Weekly* 45(7), 12–16.

Parthasarathy, B. (2001). *India Subdivision Monsoon Rainfall Data*. Pune: Indian Institute of Tropical Meteorology.

Parthasarathy, B., A. A. Munot, and D. R. Kothawale (1994). "All-India monthly and seasonal rainfall series: 1871–1993." *Theoretical and Applied Climatology* 49(4), 217–24.

Parthasarathy, B., A. A. Munot, and D. R. Kothawale (1995). "Monthly and seasonal rainfall series for all-India homogeneous regions and meteorological subdivisions: 1871–1994." In *Contributions from Indian Institute of Tropical Meteorology* (RR-065). Pune: Indian Institute of Tropical Meteorology.

Perreault, Thomas (2003). "Changing places: Transnational networks, ethnic politics, and community development in the Ecuadorian Amazon." *Political Geography* 22(1), 61–88.

Peters, Margaret E. (2015). "Open trade, closed borders: Immigration in the era of globalization." *World Politics* 67(1), 114–54.

Plant, Roger (2002). "Latin America's multiculturalism: Economic and agrarian dimensions." In *Multiculturalism in Latin America*, ed. Rachel Sieder. London: Palgrave Macmillan, pp. 208–26.

Posner, Daniel N. (2005). *Institutions and Ethnic Politics in Africa*. New York, NY: Cambridge University Press.

Potts, Deborah (2012). "Challenging the myths of urban dynamics in Sub-Saharan Africa: The evidence from Nigeria." *World Development* 40 (7), 1382–93.

Ramos, Alcida Rita (2002). "Cutting through state and class: Sources and strategies of self-representation in Latin America." In *Indigenous Movements, Self-Representation, and the State in Latin America*, ed. Kay B. Warren and Jean E. Jackson. Austin, TX: University of Texas Press, pp. 251–79.

Rice, Robert, and Donna Lee Van Cott (2006). "The Emergence and performance of indigenous peoples' parties in South America." *Comparative Political Studies* 39(6), 709–32.

Riker, William H. (1964). *Federalism: Origin, Operation, Significance*. Boston, MA: Little, Brown.

Rodden, Jonathan A. (2005). *Hamilton's Paradox: The Promise and Peril of Fiscal Federalism*. Cambridge: Cambridge University Press.

Roeder, Philip G. (2009). "Ethnofederalism and the mismanagement of conflicting nationalisms." *Regional & Federal Studies* 19(2), 203–19.

Rose, Elaina (2001). "Ex-ante and ex-post labor supply response to risk in a low-income area." *Journal of Development Economics* 64(2), 371–88.

Ross, Cameron (2014). "Regional elections and electoral malpractice in Russia: The manipulation of electoral rules, voters, and votes." *Region* 3(1), 147–72.

Salehyan, Idean (2011). *Rebels without Borders: Transnational Insurgencies in World Politics*. Ithaca, NY: Cornell University Press.

Sarsons, Heather (2015). "Rainfall and conflict: A cautionary tale." *Journal of Development Economics* 115, 62–72.

Satterthwaite, David (2008). "Understanding Asian cities: A synthesis of the findings from eight city case studies." *Global Urban Development Magazine* 4(2), 1–24.

Sawyer, Suzana (1997). "The 1992 Indian mobilization in lowland Ecuador." *Latin American Perspectives* 24(3), 65–82.

Schaible, Damian S. (2001). "Life in Russia's 'closed city': Moscow's movement restrictions and the rule of law." *NYU Law Review* 76(1), 344–74.

Scheve, Kenneth F., and Matthew J. Slaughter (2001). *Globalization and the Perceptions of American Workers*. New York, NY: Cambridge University Press.

Seymour, Lee J. M. (2010). "The regional politics of the Darfur crisis." In *The International Politics of Mass Atrocities: The Case of Darfur*, ed. David R. Black and Paul D. Williams. New York, NY: Routledge, pp. 49–67.

Shaver, Andrew, and Yang-Yang Zhou (2017). "Do Refugees Spread or Reduce Conflict?." Manuscript, Princeton University, Princeton, NJ.

Solinger, Dorothy J. (2014). "The modalities of geographic mobility in China and their impacts, 1980–2010." In *China-India: Pathways of Economic and Social Development*, ed. Delia Davin and Barbara Harriss-White (vol. 193 of the *Proceedings of the British Academy*). Oxford: Oxford University Press, pp. 3–27.

South, Scott J., Katherine Trent, and Sunita Bose (2014). "Skewed sex ratios and criminal victimization in India." *Demography* 51(3), 1019–40.

Stedman, Stephen John, and Fred Tanner, eds. (2003). *Refugee Manipulation: War, Politics, and the Abuse of Human Suffering*. Washington, DC: Brookings Institution Press.

Stocks, Anthony (2005). "Too much for too few: Problems of indigenous land rights in Latin America." *Annual Review of Anthropology* 34(1), 85–104.

Swain, Ashok (1993). "Conflicts over water: The Ganges water dispute." *Security Dialogue* 24(4), 429–39.

Thachil, Tariq (2017). "Do rural migrants divide ethnically in the city? Evidence from an ethnographic experiment in India." *American Journal of Political Science* 61(4), 908–26.

The Hunger Project (2014). *2014 State of Participatory Democracy Report.* New York, NY: United Nations Democracy Fund.

Thieme, Susan (2014). "Coming home? Patterns and characteristics of return migration in Kyrgyzstan." *International Migration* 52(5), 127–43.

Tiebout, Charles M. (1956). "A pure theory of local expenditures." *Journal of Political Economy* 64(5), 416–24.

Tock, Andrea (2011). "Q'eqchís vs. Chabil Utzaj: La Batalla Continúa." *Plaza Pública*, August 6, available at www.plazapublica.com.gt/content/qeqchis-vs-chabil-utzaj-la-batalla-continua (accessed October 10, 2017).

TOI News Service (1986a). "Delhi fears post-riot migrations." *Times of India.* October 28, p. 1.

TOI News Service (1986b). "Migrants turn violent in Delhi: Call for Punjab bandh today." *Times of India*, October 27, p. 1.

Treisman, Daniel (2007). *The Architecture of Government: Rethinking Political Decentralization.* Cambridge: Cambridge University Press.

UNDP (2009). *Human Development Report 2009: Overcoming Barriers – Human Mobility and Development.* New York, NY: United Nations Development Program.

United Nations (2014). *World Urbanization Prospects: 2014 Revision.* New York, NY: United Nations, Department of Economic and Social Affairs, Population Division.

US Department of State (2016). *Country Reports on Human Rights Practices for 2016: Russia.* United States Department of State, Bureau of Democracy, Human Rights and Labor, Washington, DC, available at www.state.gov /documents/organization/265678.pdf (accessed October 11, 2017).

US Department of the Army (2003). *Country Studies.* US Department of the Army, Washington, DC, available at http://countrystudies.us/ (accessed October 16, 2107).

Van Cott, Donna Lee (2001). "Explaining ethnic autonomy regimes in Latin America." *Studies in Comparative International Development* 35(4), 30–58.

Van Cott, Donna Lee (2003). "Institutional change and ethnic parties in South America." *Latin American Politics and Society* 45(2), 1–39.

Verma, Monika (2011). "Return of the politics of nativism in Maharashtra." *Indian Journal of Political Science* 72(2), 747–58.

Vortherms, Samantha (2017). "Between the center and the people: Localized citizenship in China". Ph.D. thesis, University of Wisconsin–Madison.

Wallace, Jeremy (2013). "Cities, redistribution, and authoritarian regime survival." *Journal of Politics* 75(3), 632–45.

Weiner, Myron (1978). *Sons of the Soil: Migration and Ethnic Conflict in India.* Princeton, NJ: Princeton University Press.

Wilkinson, Steven I. (2004). *Votes and Violence: Electoral Competition and Ethnic Riots in India*. New York, NY: Cambridge University Press.

Williamson, Jeffrey G. (1998). "Globalization, labor markets and policy backlash in the past." *Journal of Economic Perspectives* 12(4), 51–72.

World Bank (2009). *World Development Report 2009: Reshaping Economic Geography*. Washington, DC: World Bank.

Yashar, Deborah J. (1999). "Democracy, indigenous movements, and the post-liberal challenge in Latin America." *World Politics* 52(1), 76–104.

Zhu, Yu, Martin Bell, Sabine Henry, and Michael White (2013). "Rural-urban linkages and the impact of internal migration in Asian developing countries." *Asian Population Studies* 9(2), 119–23.

# Acknowledgments

We are grateful to David Stasavage for helping shape this manuscript and an anonymous referee for detailed comments. Thanks also to Scott Abramson, William Ascher, Shane Barter, Isabelle Côté, Matthew Mitchell, Jack Paine, Scott Straus, Monica Toft, Chagai Weiss, participants at the University of Wisconsin–Madison Comparative Politics Colloquium, at the Pacific Basin Research Center Working Group on Governance and Internal Migration, and in Scott Straus's graduate seminar on political violence for feedback. We are grateful to Roberta Rice for sharing data. We thank Martin Bell for making available migration data from the IMAGE repository and Priyadarshi Amar and Emily VanMeter for excellent research assistance. Bhavnani is grateful for research support from the University of Wisconsin–Madison, and Lacina is grateful for research support from the University of Rochester.

# Political Economy

## David Stasavage
*New York University*
David Stasavage is Julius Silver Professor in the Wilf Family Department of Politics at New York University. He previously held positions at the London School of Economics and at Oxford University. His work has spanned a number of different fields and currently focuses on two areas: development of state institutions over the long run and the politics of inequality. He is a member of the American Academy of Arts and Sciences.

### About the Series
The Element Series Political Economy provides authoritative contributions on important topics in the rapidly growing field of political economy.

Elements are designed so as to provide broad and in depth coverage combined with original insights from scholars in political science, economics, and economic history. Contributions are welcome on any topic within this field.

# Cambridge Elements ≡

# Political Economy

---

## Elements in the Series

*State Capacity and Economic Development: Present and Past*
Mark Dincecco

*Nativism and Economic Integration Across the Developing World: Collision and Accommodation*
Rikhil R. Bhavnani and Bethany Lacina

A full series listing is available at: www.cambridge.org/EPEC

Printed in the United States
By Bookmasters